Johnny's U.S. Open

Golf's Sacred Journey 2

A Novel By

David L. Cook, Ph.D.

Foreword by
Tom Lehman

Johnny's U.S. Open
Golf's Sacred Journey 2

By David L. Cook, PH.D.
Foreword by Tom Lehman

www.LinksofUtopia.com

Published by Sacred Journey Stories

ISBN 978-0-9742650-6-3

Printed in the United States of America
First Printing, August 2013

Cover Photograph by Hattie Barham
Cover Design by Nathan Stufflebean

Contents:

Endorsements

"David Cook has a way of reaching into those places where all the pain and shame are stored for the purpose of letting God take them away for good. The truths in this book have touched my heart and inspired me to be all in for God's purpose. I hope and pray that they have the same impact on you."

Tom Lehman, British Open Champion 1996, U.S. Ryder Cup Captain 2006

"Dr. Cook has been a mentor of mine for 20 years. He inspires all of us to dream big. *Johnny's U.S. Open* touches the golfer's heart and soul in unexpected ways. In his first book we were coached to bury the lies that hold us back in life. In this sequel you will be inspired to plant 'dream seed' that will usher you into your destiny in golf and life."

Major Dan Rooney, PGA – Founder, Folds of Honor and the Patriot Golf Club, Tulsa Oklahoma

"Once again, David Cook's story telling ability is incredible. He creatively weaves together golf lessons and life lessons from a heavenly perspective. Fear is a common theme in our lives. *Johnny's U.S. Open* coaches us to overcome fear's grip and discover "freedom in the chaos" especially on game day. "

Hall Sutton, 1983 PGA Championship Champion and PGA Tour Player of the Year, Ryder Cup Captain, 2004

● Endorsements ●

"Dr. Cook's second book, *Johnny's U.S. Open*, is as great if not even greater than the first. It takes the reader even deeper into Truth. It confronts man's ancient enemy: fear. Its lessons release us from fear's prison into freedom's brilliant light."

Jim Hardy, 2007 National PGA Teacher of the Year, Best-Selling Author, Top 10 Golf Instructor -- Golf Digest

"David Cook has done it again with *Johnny's U.S. Open*! He has a gift for telling a story that captivates your interest. You can't wait to turn the page. He paints vivid word pictures that illustrate not only nature's beauty, but life lessons based on God's unchanging truth. If you enjoyed Dr. Cook's first book, you won't want to miss reading the rest of the story. I loved it and know you will, too!"

Scott Simpson, U.S. Open Champion, 1987

"*Johnny's U.S. Open* is jam packed with spiritual nuggets inspiring us to be strong and courageous along the path of our faith journey. David Cook once again strums the longing chords God has placed in our hearts."

Bill Rogers, 1981 British Open Champion and PGA Tour Player of the Year

"*Johnny's U.S. Open* has changed the intentions of my heart. The concept of "dream-guardian" has awakened a dream seed within my soul.

Tom Woods, Executive Vice President, Colliers International, Retail Properties

"I've known David Cook for a long time. It doesn't surprise me that he continues to communicate and inspire so effectively. By helping you to reflect on your personal journey, *Johnny's U.S. Open* will lead you down the path to true greatness."

David Robinson, NBA MVP, 1992 Olympic Gold Medalist, Two-Time World Champion

"David Cook takes us back to Utopia in an even more in depth and sophisticated light than we've ever seen before. We journey deeper into our relationship with Johnny and get to know his history and teachings from the core. The book is filled with wonderful new characters and sub-plots while expanding on all the teachings of our first trip to Utopia. I'm excited to grab my clubs and find my own Freedom in the Chaos!"

Matthew Dean Russell, Director: Seven Days in Utopia

Dr. Cook has been one of my dream guardians for the last few years. His teaching has taught me to have freedom in the chaos. This book transcends golf and teaches us to be "noticers" in the game of life. As I play, Dr. Cook has encouraged me to be a "noticer" inside the ropes of the Tour. I know that *Johnny's U.S. Open* will open your eyes to freedom, dreams, and the pursuit of your ultimate destiny."

Billy Hurley III, Professional Golfer

Dedication

To all my golf instructors and golf sport psychology mentors through the years: Johnny Arreaga, Howard Nelson, Bob Rotella, Dick Coop, Rick McGuire, Jim Hardy, Stan Utley, Bryan Gathright, Michael Lamanna, Dana Bellanger, Randy Towner, Jim Wilkinson, Tim Berg, Chuck Cook, Dick Harmon, Bruce Summerhays, Laird Small, Emil Hale, Mike Vardeman, Wayne Peddy, Robert Powers, and Rick Acton.

Acknowledgements

To my captivating wife Karen and my two girls, Lexie and Hannah who inspire me to write and contemplate life deeply.

To all my friends in Utopia, a place for which my heart continually yearns. I especially want to thank my friend Robert Sullivan for encouraging the dreams of all the sojourners that visit *Utopia Golf* and the *Buried Lies Cemetery*.

To Tracy Hillis and Jan Blalock, the heart and face of the *Links of Utopia Ministries* in Utopia.

To Scott Simpson, Tom Lehman, and Jim Hardy for reading and editing the original manuscript and adding wisdom and insight from an "inside the ropes" perspective. And to Liz Worley and Karen Cook for your tedious copy-editing.

To Donnie Walsworth and all my friends at Walsworth Publishing for donating time, expertise, energy and resources to bring life to this project.

To my late Grandaddy "Joe Joe" who took me under his wing in the summers on the golf courses and rivers of Arkansas and Grandmother Lucile who spoiled us with her cooking after golf and fishing.

And to my dad and mom, Charles and Dodie, who gave me a love for golf and God. And my two brothers, Dan and King, who love to tee it up with me and trash talk all 19 holes.

• Acknowledgements •

And finally to my best friend Jesus, who paints an "Obra Maestra" with our lives.

Foreword:

By Tom Lehman

A few months ago I received a message from David Cook letting me know he had just finished writing the sequel to his first book, *Golf's Sacred Journey*, which was subsequently made into the movie, *Seven Days in Utopia*. He wanted to know if I would read it and give him some feedback from a player's perspective. As a huge fan of his and someone who was inspired and moved by the first book, I could not wait to pick up where Johnny, Travis and our nameless young golfer had left off. Where that was, exactly, was the 72nd hole of the Texas Open. The unknown mini tour journeyman had a birdie putt to stunningly upset the world's number one player. The book ended with the putt rolling towards the hole. I, like you, was left in suspense wondering whether or not it went in. We all have wondered. And so the sequel begins by addressing the question: "Did he make the putt?"

The first thing that connected with me this second time around was Dr. Cook's answer to that question. I wanted to know whether the putt went in or not, to know whether to celebrate, or not. While he answers the question in the context of the new story, in the introduction he challenges us first. He poses a question to the question instead… "does it really matter." It caused me pause and reflect: "Does it really matter?"

The question made me think of the time a few years ago when I was the captain of the US Ryder Cup Team. I had the opportunity to pick the brain of a man whom I had admired from afar for a long,

long time: Coach John Wooden. I was blessed to be able to visit
Coach Wooden for three hours in the privacy of his home, just he and
I. He said so many things that day that I will never forget. One of the
overriding themes that came across loud and clear was his perspective
on performance. His definition of success was not built around "who
made the putt." Coach's definition had to do with whether or not you
had done all that was in your power to be the best you could be with
the talent that you had.

As I thought about Coach's definition of success, and Dr. Cook's
question, it occurred to me that it only mattered "if he made the putt
or not" if Luke (the name given to our young golfer in this new story)
had not done all that he could possibly do to prepare for that moment.
If failing in the biggest moments of life is a result of not doing all
you can do to be at your best when your best is needed, then knowing
whether it went in or not means a great deal.

The flip side is all about the perspective that Dr. Cook is trying to
get across and that John Wooden embraced. If you have done all you
can to prepare, and you do stand up to that putt with confidence and
commitment, and with all the pressure on your shoulders you do give
it the very best that you have, and if you approach it with courage,
then you have already won the battle. The results are not the barome-
ter of success. True success is the inner knowledge that you were fully
committed in word and deed to becoming the best you could possibly
be.

With that issue settled in my mind I dove into Johnny's U.S.
Open. As significant as that first question was to me, the real power of
David's sequel has to do with vision. He calls it our dream seed.

Over the past ten or twenty years, I have consistently witnessed
lives that have become train wrecks. This is not to say that my life has
not been without its own version of crash and burn episodes, because

it has. We all have them in one way or another. When I know what I know about my own life, and when I see what I see on TV, or in the paper, or hear on the radio about how someone has just done the most horrific thing, it always causes me to pause and think about what went wrong? How did it happen? How is it possible to begin where we began with the innocence of youth and the hope of the future and end up with others in a pile up of derailed dreams?

Johnny's U.S. Open has connected with me because I believe we all have a vision, a dream, of who we want to be. We all have a dream and a hope of being that person we know we can be, of who we long to be. I believe a loving God, who has given us all differing talents to be used to the best of our ability, created us all uniquely. So much of the guilt that we carry is a result of knowing just how far we have wandered from that vision of who we wish we were. There is so much pain in this world because the things we dreamed of as kids, the lives we wanted to live, have long been forgotten. We have wandered so far off of the path and so far from what we once knew to be right. We are tempted to consider ourselves and our dreams to be hopeless, a lost cause. If we give in we have given up the fight.

Dr. Cook makes it very clear that there is good news for us all. There is love, forgiveness and acceptance offered to us by the God of the universe, a God who is all about second chances, mulligans and restarts. The God who sent His son, Jesus, to this earth is the God who wants to restore that vision and dream in our lives. It is never too late with God, and it is never too late with those who love us. It is my hope that this book becomes a vehicle in all of our lives that leads to restoration with our creator and a renewed vision of who we were put on this earth to be and the courage to chase it.

It is a blessing for me to be a small part of this second journey with David Cook and with you. It is a journey worth taking, a journey that includes falls and hard knocks, and most importantly a journey

12

of getting up off the ground and continuing on. Like the title says, because God is in charge of it, because He ultimately writes the script, it
is a Sacred Journey, and I am grateful to be on it with you. God bless
you all!

Introduction

I ended the first book (and movie) of this series, *Seven Days in Utopia* (original title of the book: *Golf's Sacred Journey: Seven Days at the Links of Utopia*) without the reader knowing if the golfer made the putt to win the Texas Open. I purposely left this to the imagination to encourage the reader to consider the deeper issues of the heart. My initial answer to the inevitable question of whether he made the putt was: "Does it really matter?"

As I contemplated the writing of a sequel, I knew I would need to address the question, since its answer would determine the direction of this story. I started the sequel journey with a single, stand-alone chapter that answered the question. To start with, I posted it on my website for the curious. But this new stand-alone chapter didn't fit at the end of the first book. Neither did it fit at the start of the second. So what to do?

I decided to use this chapter as a "bridge" between the two books. I chose to film a reading of this "bridge chapter" in the Waresville Cemetery in Utopia, Texas. This cemetery is located in the center of the *Links of Utopia* golf course and was the location of the defining Easter morning cemetery scene in the book and movie. I posted my reading of the chapter on the website as an open invitation to anyone who wanted to continue their journey and "bury their lies" in the *Buried Lies Cemetery* in Utopia, Texas.

I could not have imagined what would happen next. Over one million people have gone to the website *didhemaketheputt.com* after

14

reading the book or watching the movie. Thousands have sent their buried lies for us to bury in Utopia. We continue to receive hundreds per month. We have witnessed hundreds more who have made a trek to Utopia to personally bury their lies and explore the *Links of Utopia* golf course and movie sites.

I encourage you, before you start this book, to go to the website *didhemaketheputt.com*, view the short reading of the bridge chapter, bury your lies, then return here to continue the journey with Chapter 1. In case you don't have a computer or Internet access, I have included the bridge chapter just before the first chapter of the sequel.

Finally, if you have not read the first book, please take the time to start your journey there. Like most Hollywood movies adapted from a book, the storylines of the book and movie are significantly different. When faced with the decision to write a sequel to the screenplay or book, I chose the book. I wrote it as if the movie had never been made. For example, in the movie Johnny is an elderly divorced recovering alcoholic with no children. In the book Johnny is a middle-aged married man with a delightful family that you will meet within these pages. I also took the liberty of adapting a couple of themes from the screenplay that will help the story of this book unfold. Therefore don't be surprised when you read about the Obra Maestra, a theme that appeared in the movie but not in the first book.

Should you need one, your copy of the first book is available at *linksofutopia.com*.

• Johnny's U.S. Open •

The "Bridge" Chapter: Did He Make the Putt?

I heard my name over the makeshift loudspeakers as the tournament director hoisted the trophy in my direction. In the midst of this surreal scene of crazed underdog fans mixed with those disappointed by the fall of their champion, I reached for the trophy feeling like both a hero and a villain. I was being anointed by a world obsessed with putting people on a pedestal.

Johnny said that when a man is put on that pedestal, unbeknownst to him, he accepts the public scrutiny that comes with the inevitable great fall. He taught me that we live and perform on a stage before a sick, voyeuristic paparazzi media hiding in the shadows of each tragic demise.

It was one week ago in the cemetery on Easter Sunday that Johnny had helped me understand that no man was made for a pedestal. He explained how that spot had been reserved before the beginning of time for One. No man can carry the weight of glory, nor is he supposed to. We talked about how all champions fall when talent fails to hold up under the pressure or when age or death eventually prevails in this mortal state. And when it happens, early or late, another is anointed and the cycle proceeds. There is nothing so sad as watching a champion fade. A. E. Housman in his poem "To an Athlete Dying Young" said it best:

> "Now you will not swell the rout
> Of lads that wore their honors out,
> Runners whom renown outran

And the name died before the man."

Sensing the birth of a revolution because of my break with tradition on the final putt, the crowd erupted in raucous applause as my fingers touched the cool, polished bronze boot that served as the crown at this, a most unsuspected coronation. Wasn't I just an average kid from central Texas? Wasn't it just two weeks ago that I was just another nameless face on the mini tours immersed in a devastating crash-and-burn scene? What I discovered was that to a world starved for a hero, anonymity served as the seed of hope. In anonymity there is no disqualifying baggage, no sense of mortality in the emerging king.

At that moment life stood still as I contemplated deeply what had just happened. Life sometimes turns on a razor's edge; for me it had been a fork in the road. So often at day's end we stare at the back of the tapestry of our lives trying to make sense of the meaningless meanderings of the thread. And then one day it happens. Through a messenger or experience we hear the clear voice of God calling us to take a peek at the other side of the tapestry. And when we do we are undone by the beauty of the story being woven. And the meaning of a life of inconsequential coincidences emerges into an epic adventure with a purpose and calling worth living for.

The microphone was handed to me and the potential revolutionaries awaited their call. In an instant my words had weight. Never before had my words carried much meaning. I had a moment to think. What could I say that would serve as seed for their journey? Anxiety crept in and cotton hung thick from the roof of my mouth.

Then, just as I was about to speak, I heard the distinct call of a flock of geese overhead. As I looked up I couldn't help but wonder why they were so late in their migration north. And then I heard the Voice, the same Voice I had experienced when I heard the knock of destiny on the green. The Voice simply said, "Tell the crowd what you see."

A peace settled over me, and these words streamed forth, feeling like a cool drink of water from a heavenly source: "When I was a kid, I loved the sounds of spring. I would lie in the emerging green grass with my dog staring into the sky, hoping to catch a glimpse and sound of geese heading north. They would fly in formation on their quest to find a nest for the birth of the next generation. One goose always led in the V formation, while all the others flew in the wake of his lead."

At this, the honk of the geese trumpeted loudly, causing everyone to turn their heads skyward. I paused to let the moment set in.

I continued, "There may be no tradition greater than an innate urge to migrate in the early spring. It is obvious these geese have broken tradition. Though they may seem late, nevertheless they have a destiny. So do you and I.

"Today, I will take the lead in another unconventional migration, knowing that this victory may inspire others in my wake. However, I will not receive the champion's pedestal. I am but a child of the One who carries the title of Champion.

"Two weeks ago I was an also-ran on the mini tours, immersed in one of the greatest collapses of my life. I choked my guts out. In an attempt to escape, I drove deep into the Hill Country of Texas, eventually coming upon a fork in the road. I chose to turn left toward the small village of Utopia, not knowing that it would change my life.

"At sunset that evening I met a man named Johnny who called me out, challenging me to be a revolutionary. I spent a week with him, emerging with a new heart. While he taught me the lost wisdom of the game, the most significant thing he did was to introduce me to a new voice in my life -- the Voice of the true migration.

"I don't know how to say this well because I am new at this. But this victory was the start of a revolution for me. When I took out the Face-On putter for the final putt, it was a symbol for what had been birthed in my soul in Utopia. From this day forward I will never follow tradition for tradition's sake. Instead, I endeavor to follow but one voice, and that is the Voice of truth. Secondly, I refuse to play for acceptance, because excellence is my coach.

"In closing I know that there are two reasons for this victory. One is because I flew in the wake of Johnny's wisdom. The second is because I knelt before the Champion's throne in a cemetery far from this place. It was in this posture that I received my true purpose in life and the grace to bury the lies that had a choke hold on my talent. When you walk in your purpose, a trophy pales in comparison to the fruit of your wake."

I held the trophy toward heaven and the geese overhead and said, "Let the revolution begin!"

Chapter 1

Life is a sacred journey. It is a trek where a meltdown can precede greatness, where common strangers emerge as pathfinders, where a fork in the road can change a destiny, and where grace abounds for the perceptive. Around every bend of this circuitous adventure modern-day parables are revealed to the noticer and often a name is more than a name. It is sacred because its true mission is to catalyze a revolution of the soul. My victory in the Texas Open six weeks ago was proof of these eternal truths.

The first few weeks on this revolutionary path were extraordinary. While I played well and had four top-thirty finishes, it wasn't my play that I will remember the most. It was the addictive force of soul freedom. I was captivated by the power and transforming impact of the dual meaning of SFT. SFT defined the purpose of every shot I hit: see it, feel it, trust it. SFT also defined my life's purpose: see His face, feel His presence, trust His love. Johnny's brilliance set me on a revolutionary path with three letters of the alphabet.

Others noticed and wanted what I had. I had a new platform and relished the chance to offer direction to the searcher. Pilots are called to a narrow heading when landing a plane. What I found was that the call to true north for many was too narrow. But more than a few received it and grabbed hold of the depth of its power. When they did, life stood still for me. Fulfillment went deep, as did my breath.

Until a few weeks ago, my breath was eternally shallow, a prisoner of the prey's fear. I had been stuck with a meandering purpose and a life of unsettling prospects. The fear of failure haunted me. But now I was a player in the game of life. Because of that, I was emerging as a player in the game of golf.

With the U.S. Open looming in two and a half weeks, it was the perfect time to return to Utopia. At the conclusion of the PGA Tour's Texas swing, I used Memorial Day as an opportunity to take another trek on the glorious back roads of Texas to see my friend for a tune-up. However, I didn't know that my journey with Johnny had only just begun.

Late in the afternoon on Memorial Day after a long day's drive, I rolled up to Johnny's home. The 1930's farmhouse was nestled quaintly among the century-old live oaks that provided shade and shelter from the harsh Texas climate. An American flag flew out front. The St. Augustine grass spread its cool blades of green throughout the expansive yard shaded in part by the great arms of the oaks. Fruit-bearing trees were grouped in an orchard next to a large garden displaying their early season fruit, the tantalizing promise of things to come. The garden was surrounded by a six-foot net fence keeping the fresh supply of vegetables safe from the appetites of the deer, feral hogs, and rabbits. Fresh rows of new plantings were evident in the dark, rich dirt of the Sabinal Valley.

The house was a distinct turn-of-the-century Texas Hill Country farmhouse born of both necessity and art. All old farmhouses start as a simple rectangle then evolve: A keeping room is added to this side, a nook to that, a new porch over here, and a bedroom bump out there. That's what gives them character. Unlike the developers of urban sprawl, the early settlers built with cross breezes and sun position in mind. Porches were strategically placed to catch the warm, south-east sun on a winter morning, yet to block the cold, northwest winds of an approaching winter storm. It could be argued that the kiss of early morning sunlight was as important to the life of the kitchen and breakfast room as the smell of freshly brewed coffee.

No farmhouse was complete without a west-facing covered porch for catching the great art in the sky at the end of an honest day's work. Johnny said that the voice of heaven for a cowboy lies in the sound of wooden rocking chairs creaking on the old porch at the end of the day, the hand of his wife held close, a glass of sweet tea, and the flash of orange in the towering, anvil-shaped clouds on the distant horizon. In those sacred and silent moments "all is well," giving meaning to the words sung on Sunday mornings beneath the spires of the white frame churches. These churches, living monuments to the circuit-riding preachers of the past, form the centerpiece of small, forgotten communities in the Hill Country of Texas.

About half a football field away stood the old barn. You could see only remnants of red paint from years gone by, leaving natural wood to fend for itself against the elements of nature. Next to the barn was a round pen, the academic institution for the untrained or obstinate horse.

A cloud of dust swirled out of that pen, revealing that class was in session. The cloud of dust came from a foam-covered black stallion vying for freedom. The competition was fierce. All I could see for a few minutes was a headstrong stallion, rearing and pawing the air like Trigger in the opening scenes of an old Roy Rogers flick. In an abrupt turn of events, the stallion sensed that his posturing was having little effect. He bolted around the pen, creating a tornado-like effect in the dust. His eyes were fierce, his head cocked back, his main flowing wildly in this powerful display of supremacy. For a few moments this horse created the illusion of a one-horse Kentucky Derby. Then, like a trout about to be netted, he bucked high into the air, changing directions, stamping and snorting as if to rid his back of a spurring rodeo cowboy. I watched, mesmerized, wondering what was causing such agitation.

A miraculous scene unfolded. The stallion stood still, heaving for air, completely spent. Covered with foaming sweat, he lowered his head in submission and followed a lone figure, which up to now had been hidden by the dust storm. It was Johnny. He was carrying a six-foot bamboo pole with a red bandanna attached to the end.

The horse followed in submission about three feet behind this man. Johnny walked slowly and confidently in front of a thousand pounds of pure-bred testosterone that somehow followed with trust and submission. When he stopped, the horse stopped. When he walked, the horse walked. At one point he stopped and slowly turned. He stood, staring into the eyes of a wild stallion inches away, their noses almost touching.

He then cautiously raised the bamboo rod. The horse tensed but stayed put. He touched the horse with the bandanna, causing its head to rear. He reached up with his left hand and gently stroked the face of the horse, bringing calmness to its spirit. He continued to touch the quivering horse with the pole and bandanna, brushing it along its back, legs, and withers.

His gaze never left the horse, building trust between two creatures of different natures. Finally, he dropped the bamboo and raised both hands to gently rub and embrace the face of the horse.

Somehow I reached the fence unnoticed. The intensity of his focus had made me invisible. Every muscle in the horse began to loosen. His fear lessened. When his fear lessened, so did his anger, his first line of defense.

Johnny slowly picked up an antique-looking leather halter that was hanging on the fence and carefully placed it over its head and ears. He fastened it and turned to lead the compliant horse around the pen. He was living life fully committed to who he was and his purpose. He was more than a golf pro; he had learned the ways of a horseman.

He noticed me and gave me a smile and nod while remaining focused on his task. He walked the stallion around the pen then tied it to the fence. He reached for his bamboo rod and gently lifted it to the horse. At this movement the horse erupted with a jerk of its head and a kick that would have sent someone to the moon. It began to buck fiercely and uncontrollably as the leather seemed it would break. Johnny raised his hands high, standing like granite, staring the horse down like a gun fighter.

But this was no ordinary horse. This was a stallion of stallions. In one powerful thrust, the ancient leather snapped as the horse reared, tumbling backwards and onto its back. In a cloud of dust it bounded to its feet and bolted within a whisker of the horseman. The horse turned on a dime across the pen, stamped its feet, peeled its ears back, snorting as if to say, it's over.

To the shock of the horse, Johnny sprinted toward the stallion, waving the bandanna wildly. The horse, caught by surprise, began to run in circles around the pen. I jumped out of its way as it thundered past, casting foul looks and horse spit in my direction. Around and around the pen it ran. Faster and faster, working up such a lather that its hide began to turn white. All the while Johnny stood in the middle, pointing the bamboo pole with the bandanna tied to the end directly at the horse, his eyes never leaving the stallion. His smile was gone, and the look of business was on his face. The dust storm returned, and the game was on again. He would periodically cut the horse off at the pass, causing him to turn wildly, spraying dirt as its haunches hunkered in the turn exploding with the power of a howitzer in the opposite direction.

Eventually the horse stopped, lowered its head, and stamped the ground, making wild sounds and gestures as if to say, I am about to run you down. Johnny then lowered the pole and turned his back on the bluffing stallion. The stallion had a choice: Follow or remain obstinate. It remained obstinate. After Johnny walked about five steps, he peered over his shoulder at the stubborn horse, who thought it had won. Johnny turned on a dime and charged the horse with the bandanna pointed right at its face. Off to the races again.

This happened several more times, until the horse figured out he had met his match. About 30 minutes into this epic battle, Johnny turned from the horse. The horse, to my amazement, began to follow him around the round pen. It got within three feet of him and stayed on his heels. Then he stopped, and the scene I had witnessed earlier happened again: He came nose to nose with the heaving animal, stroked its face with his left hand, while rubbing the pole and bandanna all around the body. He dropped the pole and patted both sides of the horse's face. He then grabbed what was left of the halter lead and turned to lead the horse on a journey to freedom.

Chapter 2

"Hey, there," the voice of Johnny rang out across the round pen, "What brings you back here so soon? I'll meet you over by the barn in a couple minutes. I need to put him in his stall."

When Johnny showed up, he shook my hand with one of those "you better be ready" rancher handshakes.

"Beautiful creature, huh?" Johnny quipped.

"The most beautiful horse I've ever seen," I replied.

"That horse has never been ridden," Johnny stated. "One of the greatest bronc horses in the history of Texas rodeo. Been all over Texas and bucked them all. Not one made it to eight on that stallion."

"Looks a little dangerous in there," I said.

"He keeps me on my toes," Johnny said with a laugh.

"What are you going to do with him?" I asked.

"Well, they retired him in a great ceremony a couple months ago and put him out to pasture," Johnny shared. "As you can imagine, not many ranchers have use for an old stallion hanging out on their place, bullying other horses. But God gave me a heart for these rodeo has-beens. I love transforming rodeo broncs, wild mustangs, and rescued horses. Teaches me a lot about working with people, teaches me a

27

lot about me. Makes me a better instructor at whatever I'm teaching. Unlike the old term cowboys used to use, I don't break horses, I free them, turning them into trail horses for kids. The owner's a good friend. He used to be a range rat at my club in Houston. Gave him a lot of lessons. He and I thought this horse would be the ultimate test; so far we're right! He just wants to continue to use him as a breeder periodically."

Johnny continued, "After training these horses we give them to kids."

"You give bronc horses to kids?" I asked with raised eyebrows.

"No. They come here as broncs," Johnny explained with a chuckle. "They leave as freed spirits that love to be ridden. Freedom is a powerful force."

"I'm impressed! How in the world do you do it?" I asked.

"I'll save that story for later. I couldn't do it justice right now. Let's just say change requires trust, and trust leads to freedom," Johnny shared.

Johnny turned the topic back to me. "What brings you back so soon?"

In two and a half weeks I was to play in my first U.S. Open. Much of the history of the game revolved around the venerable sites of this great tournament and the names etched upon its trophy. I grew up watching the greats of the game taken out by the brutal conditions of the U.S. Open. Hands down, the scoring average in the U.S. Open was the highest of all the tournaments each year. While the greatest names in golf won many of these events, it wasn't always a pretty sight. It was a test of survival and toughness.

It could be argued that the U.S. Open was the truest championship of them all. Not only did it have the top players in the world, it also provided a comprehensive qualifying system that any good player could enter. A handful of professionals also received special exemptions. My tournament victory earned me one of those exemptions. At this point I wasn't sure if it was a good thing. It wasn't a lack of faith in my game as much as it was reality staring me in the face. I just didn't feel my game was ready. I had more to learn before I suited up.

Year after year good players limped out of this tournament, broken and embarrassed by the course and conditions. It would take months for many to recover. Many golfers' egos were as fragile as an early peach blossom. While they look good early, it takes only one spring frost to render them fruitless for the year.

Every kid who grew up playing golf dreamed of making the putt to win the U.S. Open. I was no exception. Very few get the chance to play in the tournament. Fewer still show up prepared. In the end a putt to win happens for a very few, most to never have the opportunity again. I had no idea if I would ever have the chance to play in another U.S. Open after this one. I was determined to show up ready for anything. I was preparing for the conditions, the weather, the pressure, and the final putt for victory, should it come my way. Thus I came to Johnny for some answers. I was hoping to learn a few pieces of missing information and then fly out to the Memorial, Jack's tournament, armed with the confidence I was missing.

"I'm not ready," I said, surprised at my confession. "The U.S. Open is in two and a half weeks, and I don't feel prepared."

"You aren't," Johnny agreed without missing a beat.

"Why do you say that?" I asked.

"You're here," he said with a smile and chuckle.

"You got a point," I acknowledged with a grin.

"The U.S. Open is a step up from normal competition; it's in a different league. Extreme variables, unforeseen challenges, monumental decisions in the moment of moments," Johnny agreed. "The U.S. Open is about pinpoint accuracy and freedom in the chaos."

"Freedom in the chaos?" I questioned.

"Mental chaos has stolen more majors than players want to admit," Johnny answered. "Freedom has to trump chaos coming down the stretch. When destiny is on the line, defining moments are characterized by thought freedom, meltdowns by mental chaos."

He motioned toward the round pen as he continued. "That is what the round pen has taught me. There is always a choice. You can run from or to the bandanna. That's God's way; it never changes throughout life. Every day we have to step in faith in the face of adversity rather than run in fear. We must trust the one who says, I am with you and will never forsake you."

I knew I was where I needed to be. A serenity came over me as I listened to Johnny, a humble man who sees with the eyes of faith.

"Here's a verse from the book of James that I often think about," Johnny said. "Count it pure joy whenever you face trials of many kinds, because you know that the testing of your faith develops perseverance. Perseverance must finish its work before you may be mature and complete, not lacking anything."

Whereas I might have been reluctant to listen to scripture when I first met him, Johnny had earned my trust over those first seven days in Utopia. I was hungry for all that he knew. It was food for my soul. I had been starving for years and just didn't know it.

This verse didn't seem logical, and it certainly wasn't how I reacted to adversity in my life. Happiness always came from good things, comfortable things, pleasant things. Joy just didn't seem to be associated with adversity.

"Son, let me pose a question. Do you want to be a mature and complete player?" he asked.

"Absolutely," I replied.

"Well, then, it's simple. Adversity is strewn along the path that takes you there. It makes your roots go deep. Challenge is the unexpected gift on the way to being mature and complete," Johnny revealed. "It's this uncommon perspective that provides freedom in the chaos. Very few competitors really get this."

"See that weeping willow over there by the barn?" Johnny asked as he pointed to a massive and mature tree with its elegant branches dangling in the warm sun. "I planted that for my family years ago. There's a nice rope swing hanging from one of its limbs up under the trimmed canopy. We also have a picnic table in the shade on the opposite side that we use most every day. That tree used to blow over all the time when I first planted it. I knew willows liked water so I gave it plenty not knowing that I was stunting its taproot. I had to stop giving it water and allow the root to fend for itself in the harsh conditions of the hill country. It dropped lots of leaves as its taproot went deep on a search for water, thus stabilizing the tree for the winds ahead."

Johnny paused for a moment. "The U.S. Open will go to the mature and complete."

"To win an Open, your belief roots have to go deep. You will have to face adversity over and over as it relentlessly tries to take you out. There can be no doubt in your mind that you belong there. You have to know that it is part of your destiny, though not your ultimate destiny. I believe there is more for us to discover about that this week, much more. But for now, let's start with your accuracy," he said with a definitive air about him.

"Until we narrow your variance and reel in your physical shot pattern, you will be unprepared for the Open. You see, you are playing with a modified choke dispersion, and we need a full choke pattern in the Open."

"Do you think I am good enough to compete in the Open?" I asked.

"Good enough is not in question," he said with confidence. "It's just that good enough has not emerged. It's in there; we just need to spend some time bringing it to the surface. It will take time, maybe another seven days in Utopia. We'll see."

"I've been looking forward to the Memorial later this week," I confessed.

"I don't think you can afford to play in it. In fact, I'm not sure you should play in the next two tournaments," Johnny coached. "This week is about unearthing truth. Next week is about going in a week ahead of the Open and learning the course."

"But what about the money list? What about Ryder Cup points and Tour Championship points? Skipping tournaments is giving others an advantage, isn't it?" I asked with concern.

He reached out and put his hand on my shoulder and said, "Why don't you grab your journal, head for the river, and think about your dreams. If winning a major is one of them, then meet me at the range in the morning. If not, you still have time to make it to Jack's event. Either choice is fine. Just choose one and don't ever settle for living in the middle. If you choose to stay, it will take a week. There's a room for you down at the inn if you decide to stay."

And with that he walked away.

● Johnny's U.S. Open ●

Chapter 3

The rooster's crow beat my alarm by about an hour. There was something visceral about the call, conjuring up evolutionary feelings of the adventure of a new day. It elicited both excitement and fear. Long ago the rooster, sun, moon, and seasons were the foundations of schedule. Adventures were unscheduled; they unfolded in their time.

Today there are timepieces and calendars everywhere. The pressure to meet deadlines, arrive at appointments on time, and organize the future often causes us to miss an unscheduled adventure. Many look haggard, frenzied, and on the edge of exhaustion trying to keep pace, but keep pace for what? To not get behind, to not be irresponsible, to prove their worth as they succumb to the two candles, the irascible measure of a responsible day's work. In the end, no one has time for either an unscheduled adventure or an inconvenient course correction in the middle of the sprint. Today I had a choice. I gave the rooster the nod and set off once again on an unscheduled sacred journey.

Johnny met me at the range with a mess of balls and an old 1920 side-by-side Stevens 20 gauge. There were two three-by-three-foot rifle targets that were set up on the range about 15 steps from the balls. It looked as though this was more than a psychological session today.

"Good morning," he said as he handed me the shotgun. "Two targets, two shells. Let's see if you can take out the center of each target from here."

Intrigued, I aimed at the target, released the safety, and pulled the front trigger. The old Stevens bucked with an attitude as the first target was covered by a few widely dispersed BB holes. I swung to the second target, aimed, and blasted the entire center of the target, leaving a 10-inch gaping hole.

"Wow," I said. "What was the difference in the shells?"

"Nothing," Johnny said, "The difference is in the choke. The first barrel was set at modified choke, the second was full choke. The old side-by-sides were made so that the shooter could choose which dispersion met the challenge he faced: front trigger wide and short, or back trigger narrow and long. Your current golf dispersion, or accuracy, is set at modified choke and we need to tighten it up to full choke for the U.S. Open and beyond. More BBs concentrated on the center of the target."

I handed Johnny the shotgun as he asked me to hit a lob wedge to a pin about 30 yards away. As I did, Johnny blasted the ball out of the air, scaring me to death as I was unaware that he had reloaded the gun.

"Modified choke," he said with a hearty laugh as my heart recovered from the surprise.

He then asked me to hit a pitching wedge to the 130 flag. I was ready this time. He blasted that ball out of the air at about 70 yards.

"Full choke," he deadpanned.

"Ok, let's see you take it to the top and stop."

I was still contemplating the shotgun lesson, but Johnny was a step in front.

"Six-iron ok for this?" I asked.

Instead of answering, he nodded. Then he looked at me with the warmth of a grandfather and said, "I'm glad you chose to stay." He stretched out his hand and affectionately squeezed my neck with that catcher's mitt of a paw, looked into my eyes and continued: "In the next ten minutes you'll have to make that decision again."

He backed off, giving me space to take a few warm-up swings to limber up.

"You made a courageous decision in the Texas Open when you pulled out the Face-On putter to sink the final putt. It was a brave move, filled with conviction." He paused as he kicked a ball out of the pile for me to hit, then continued. "But that was only the first step. The next ten minutes will determine if you have what it takes."

"For what?" I quickly asked.

"To revolutionize the high-jump like Dick Fosbury, to kick the first side-on field goal like Pete Gogolak, to throw the first forward pass like Bradbury Robinson, to shoot the first jump-shot like Johnny Cooper, to compete with the two-handed backhand like Chris Evert, or to shoot an underhand free-throw like Rick Berry," he paused then continued. "This is more than a golf lesson; this is about choice. A choice that can change your destiny... a choice that can change how the game is played. It's a decision that will have to face the fury of 300 years of tradition."

"All I want is to decrease my shot variance. You talk as if I am going to change history," I questioned.

"You just might," Johnny replied with a sly grin.

"And who are all those people?" I asked.

"Tradition breakers … courageous performance revolutionaries … athlete artists," Johnny spoke in a reverent tone. "Change is uncomfortable for many to accept, especially if it goes against the accepted teaching or coaching of the day. Tradition breakers push the envelope. When they do, they push buttons."

Johnny paused then spoke as a prophet. "And those buttons often provoke anger, disgust, slander, and hatred."

Getting more than I bargained for, I simply asked, "You want me to go to the top and stop?"

"Yep," he nodded.

I made my backswing and held the position at the top.

Johnny looked at my position. Then he asked me what was good about it.

"O.K., my wrists are hinged, the back of my left hand is flat, my left arm is straight, and I am on plane with my arms and club face. My upper body has rotated rather than swayed, and my weight is still on the inside of my right foot. This is the slot I have to get into to have my shot work."

"Why did you take it to the top as you did?" Johnny asked, catching me off guard once again.

"What do you mean?" I asked, hoping to buy some time.

"You swung the club back, hoping your arms would pronate just the right amount to get your hands in position to hinge just right allowing the back of your left wrist to be flat all the while keeping your arms from running away from your body while trying to hit your plane slot. Seems like a very inefficient and unreliable way to get the club in the slot."

"It seems to work for me," I stated.

"Not really. It undermines your accuracy. It will be evident under the pressure of a U.S. Open set-up. Pressure can affect the rhythm and synchronization of all the variables. You're missing the most important variable: freedom. To win under pressure, you must maintain freedom in the chaos. If there is no freedom, there is no synchronization."

He had a point, but I didn't know where this was leading.

"I believe that somewhere in the evolution of the competitive golf swing we missed an important point. The point is freedom during the chaos, intensity, and interference of game day. It is mental freedom that will allow the golfer to maintain focus in front of the ball where the game is played, where a masterpiece is painted, not behind the ball, where the player is trying to manage positions with an increased heart rate and tense and agitated muscles. As tension mounts, breakdowns in synchronization are inevitable. Panic takes the mind to the backswing rather than the target. Great players crash and burn as they emerge on the U.S. Open leader board, but not because they are poor players. They fall because their synchronization fails. They simply can't consistently get it in the slot coming down the stretch. They lack freedom to play the game in front of their ball when it means the most.

"Is there a more efficient way to get the club in the slot, a bulletproof technique that would eliminate back swing faults? In other words, is there a way to eliminate the backswing as we know it?" he asked.

"I believe you think there is," I laughed to break up the moment.

"You ready to go on an adventure? An expedition to find a better way?" Johnny asked, choosing words that he knew would motivate me.

The word adventure had started my day. It always struck a chord with me. I have always yearned for exploration. In this world where the land has mostly been explored, our personal explorations take place in the heart and mind. This is a journey of uncharted waters for most of us, an adventure both treacherous and exhilarating. Treacherous in that we must let go of the security of false or partial truth. Exhilarating because we move to a new realm of performance, a zone seldom achieved by the status quo. It starts with the challenge of false truth and doesn't end until we one day step into eternity where the extraordinary on earth is but a footstool to magnificence.

"I'm ready," I said, knowing this was going to be a joust between fear and hope.

Johnny pulled a page from the great Harvey Penick, "All right then, figure it out. Find a better way. I'll be back in an hour."

He walked away, leaving me stranded in what felt like an Outward Bound expedition to Antarctica with a match and a space blanket. I had the U.S. Open staring me in the face, and the clock was ticking.

Chapter 4:

New discoveries always called out greatness in the explorer. Something so profound had to transpire in the soul of the adventurer that it freed them to pursue the unthinkable, a new way. And new ways often encountered turbulence. They break tradition.

As I contemplated Johnny's challenge, I realized I felt uneasy. I was out of my normal comfort zone. I had always had an external teacher laying out the plan. Whether in school or golf, I always submitted to the authority of my teacher or coach and followed their advice. I trusted their training, never questioning their words. After all, a coachable and compliant student isn't expected to question. Could it be our system has held us back? Has tradition once again trumped innovation, relegating most of us to cattle-drive status? My shallow taproot was about to go deeper.

I took the club to the top and stopped. That is when I found my first clue. I looked at my positions and adjusted them slightly to get them perfect. I thought to myself, just swing down from there. So I initiated my downswing from a perfect position at the top. I topped the ball.

Well, that didn't work. I thought to myself, maybe I can adjust to it. So I tried five more times. On the fifth try, I flushed it, and the ball flew perfectly.

Over the next half hour I hit about 50 balls, taking it to the top and stopping, adjusting everything perfectly, then swinging down from there. Interesting.

I stopped and analyzed what was happening. Two issues were evident. First, the shot was more accurate but shorter, probably losing about 10 yards. Secondly, to initiate the downswing, I had a tendency to lean forward to give some momentum to the static start. That caused the ball to be hit a little thin and to the right on a few of them.

Before I knew it, Johnny came walking up. He said, "Show me what you got."

Feeling a little self-conscious, I started in a static position from the top. Sure enough, I hit it thin and to the right.

I quickly said, "Let me try again. I can do better."

I hit the second shot pure and got a clap and smile from Johnny.

"Lost some distance, but it sure was pure," Johnny replied, seeming pleased.

"You've almost solved the problem. If you could start every swing with the club in the slot, not worrying about the backswing, the game would be easier, accuracy would be improved, and you could give more attention to the game in front of the ball."

He reached for my club. "The only issue with starting the club from the top is the loss of distance and a new tendency to lean forward to start the forward motion."

As he rolled a ball out of the pile, he continued. "You did well to create another possibility. You've opened the door to greatness. There's another way, and you've hit upon one of the elements, the pre-set. Instead of trusting your body to find the slot while in motion, you took the club to the top and then pre-set the club on the correct plane, proper wrist hinge, and appropriate amount of pronation."

Johnny took his stance to hit a shot, looked at me with a wry smile and said, "Here is the future of golf, my friend."

Without moving his arms he lifted the toe of the club straight up by hinging his wrist, keeping the back of his left wrist perfectly flat. From that position, he then pronated the toe of the club to about 45 degrees, setting it on a perfect plane. He then proceeded to turn back and through with impeccable rhythm, sending a towering draw to its destination with no loss of distance.

"I call this the Utopia Pre-Set. It is a four-count rhythm swing that takes care of getting the club in the slot in the first two moves of the backswing rather than in the last two moves. This is the key to synchronization while under pressure," Johnny said as he approached another shot. "Watch carefully. There is a purposeful rhythm to this swing. Remember rhythm, balance, and patience from your time here before?

"Yes," I responded, completely immersed in his teaching.

"The Utopia Pre-Set swing incorporates this critical element, along with removing the back swing errors caused by synchronization issues," he said as if he had a map to a hidden treasure. "Son, this is the first secret to freedom in the chaos of game day."

He set to his target, eyes painting a masterpiece. As his focus returned to the ball, he began an audible metronome-like count using the words hinge, plane, turn, turn as he striped another shot looking as though he was dancing to a four-count rhythm with a club named Ginger Rogers. He continued this dance with the future of golf for the next 10 minutes. With each shot he audibly spoke the words, holding himself accountable to an impeccable metronome like rhythm. The club effortlessly hit the slot each time. I was in awe. Never in my life had I seen such a display of complete swing control. While different-looking, the rhythm, balance, and patience of the four-count method was mesmerizing and intoxicating, a true athletic move with its own beauty.

Every lesson with Johnny went deep. There was no trite or shallow with him. He wasted no moments. Every encounter was an invitation into a defining moment for the discerning student.

"Here you go. It's your time," Johnny said with great anticipation as he handed me the club and stepped aside. "Understand this: We aren't fundamentally changing your golf swing; we are changing the synchronization or the order of a couple of the elements of the swing."

"The first key is hinging the club, with the back of your left hand remaining flat. To fade it, cup the back of your left wrist a little; to hook it, bow the back of your left wrist. With a little practice you can manipulate the ball at will. The second step is to find your desired plane. Start with 45 degrees of pronation and adjust from there to find your slot. Once your club is hinged and pronated, then the only thing left is to turn back and turn through with balance and patience. Your body knows this step. It's easy, and you've cut the synchronization factor in half. Saying the words out loud will keep you connected to the four count. It will keep you accountable to rhythm, the key to pressure golf. This swing is in essence an efficient and unique blending of the mental and physical games of golf."

He then connected the dots between the Utopia Pre-Set and SFT—see, feel, trust. "When using the conventional swing, SFT is the routine," he taught. "Now that you are graduating to the pre-set, you always start with painting the masterpiece, the see-it part. You never hit a shot without starting there. Then feel and trust are simply incorporated and defined by hinge, plane, turn, turn."

I picked up the six-iron and set it behind the ball painting the shot to my target with my eyes. With my arms straight, I then hinged my left wrist while keeping the back of my left wrist flat. Next I pronated the toe of the club to about 45 degrees, or between 1 and 2 o'clock on a clock face. Oh my, I could sense that my hands were already in the slot. This was an incredible sensation, and it was simple. Next, I simply turned to the top and turned back through the ball. I hit it a little thin but well.

Johnny grinned and nodded for me to continue. "Keep your spine angle when you hinge your wrists. You slightly lifted your upper body. The only thing that lifts is the toe of the club," he instructed.

I went through the process again. The shot flew true.

Johnny said, "Ok, say the words out loud and establish a metronome-like rhythm." He chuckled as he declared, "It's a four-count rhythm in a two-steppin' town."

I started by saying, see it, picturing a high straight ball to my target. I then started the four-count rhythm. I said the word hinge as the toe of the club lifted vertically off the ground by the simple hinging of my left wrist. I softly said plane as I pronated the toe of the club to 45 degrees, thus setting the plane of the swing. I then said turn as I turned to the top of my backswing. Finally I repeated turn as I turned through the shot, ripping a towering six-iron toward its intended destination.

I was stunned. It only took two swings to produce a perfect shot. Never have I had a lesson with such dramatic results.

While the ball was still arcing through the air, I peeked over at Johnny. His eyes were riveted on the shot like a hawk. Who was this man, unaffected by tradition, passionate about excellence?

In the end, it's fear that holds back greatness. Fear holds back genius and progress. I can sense my impending battle with fear as I contemplate incorporating the swing. Am I bold enough to give it a shot... in the U.S. Open?

"Mmmm," droned Johnny as if he were savoring a bite of coconut cream pie down at the cafe.

As the ball hit into the grassless dirt, shooting up a burst of dust on the range in Utopia, he said with a smile, "Enjoy the dance. Immerse yourself. Let go of any inhibition or fear and you will find two gifts, my friend, before sunset. I'll meet you at the horse corral in the morning. We're going to take a ride up to Obra Maestra."

"Obra what?" I called after him.

As he walked away, his shoulders jostled with laughter and he mimicked the Utopia Pre-Set swing with his left hand. "Oh, it's a painting by my favorite Western artist," he said as I stood alone, once again anticipating the adventure ahead.

"Two gifts?" I wondered.

Chapter 5

There I was, approaching my ball on the first tee of the U.S. Open. Despite the tournament official's fine baritone rendition of my name and hometown, the crowd was unimpressed, almost incredulous, that I had the audacity to take up space and time until their heroes teed it up. I walked into the shot with the confidence of a turtle embarking on a desert crossing. As I looked down the fairway in search of my target, all I could see were faces pressing into the ropes along the length of the tee box, looking back at me with smiles not knowing that they were in harm's way. The face-lined tee box looked like the hallway of a mid-century high rise.

I took my stance but had no feeling in my hands. As I looked down at the ball, I noticed that my club had morphed into a peacock feather and that I was dressed only in my boxers and black socks. The crowd erupted in laughter as I began my swing using the Utopia Pre-Set. I swung with all I had. To my horror, the ball was not influenced in the least by the wisp of the feather. I swung again and again to no avail. The crowd was rolling in laughter in the fairway as my playing partner was counting my strokes out loud.

My caddy came to my rescue with a real club, a Hogan one-iron. Legend had it that Hogan found the sweet spot once at Merion, but to this day no other golfer has. I grabbed the club like a desperate seagull going after a tossed sardine.

This time as I approached the ball, I was transported into a kitchen. The ball was at rest on a Mexican tile floor. Three feet away was the breakfast table in a cozy nook surrounded by a bay window. The spectators' contorted faces were pressed hard against the outside of the glass. They were intent on seeing my recovery shot to the coffee cup perched on the table serving as the hole. The cameraman was hanging from the overhead lighting fixture. My caddy was tending the swizzle stick that served as the pin on this treacherous par three. His patronizing comment to open the face was no help at all. A feeling of helplessness covered me as the perspiration poured down my forehead in torrents. How was I ever going to complete this shot? I collapsed into the yips. I couldn't pull the club back. Time was ticking. In the background I could hear Rod Sterling introducing the "Twilight Zone" as my childhood principal stepped into the kitchen with a paddle to assess a two-swat penalty for slow play. As he opened his drooping cellulose-laden jowls to speak, he crowed like a rooster.

My eyes opened to the caress of the glorious first light of dawn in Utopia, the suffocating fear of this U.S. Open nightmare dissipating with the daily call of the rooster from its distant perch, once again putting everything in order. My heart pulsating like the smoke stack of Engine 99, body drenched from the sweat of the prey's fear, I bolted straight up, thanking God that the nightmare was over. I made a promise to myself that no shrink would ever catch wind of that dream!

Before meeting Johnny, fear often had been the overriding theme of my dreams. But not only of my dreams, they were but a shadow of the insidious intruder that had hitched a ride on my conscious journey as well. More often than not, my life's dreams had been abandoned to fear.

By the end of my first visit to Utopia I had overcome fear by burying my lies. It was the most freeing moment of my life. To say the least, I was discouraged that fear was back knocking at the door. Breaking tradition with a new, untested swing at the U.S. Open was fertile soil for an invasion from this former resident. I was learning that each step on the journey of faith was just another battle for freedom from fear. I was determined not to let this nightmare take me down.

As I approached the corral and barn area expecting to see Johnny, I was surprised by the sight of a stunningly beautiful young woman. She was leading the great black stallion in circles with a halter lead. I also noticed for the first time that the horse had one white front foot. It looked like it was wearing a white sock. To my surprise the horse had a saddle on it. I also heard the most beautiful melodic Celtic singing as the cowgirl waltzed across her stage in Utopia oblivious to me.

After a few moments of eavesdropping on wonder, I was discovered. Instead of being embarrassed, she kept on singing as she walked in my direction, allowing the song to taper off.

"Good morning," I said as she approached.

"Johnny will be along soon," she said with a friendly smile as she turned and continued around the corral. I swear I saw the stallion smile a wry smile as if he was glad to have company in the presence of this young woman who walked with authority in her spurred and worn M.L. Leddy boots and who had two on the line now.

She came to a stop, caressed the horse's face then wrapped the halter lead around the fence near the barn. I have to admit, a shot of adrenaline struck my heart as she turned and headed directly for me. She was in control with every step she took. Her summer Stetson was tilted low as strands of blond hair swept across her face. The jingle of her spurs and sparkle of her buckle only intensified the approach of this divinely shaped blessing to the world.

She introduced herself with a handshake, "Hi, I'm Grace."

If she only knew, was my first thought.

Her handshake was anything but a dainty little squeeze. Her confident eyes, squinting in the sunlight, seemed to penetrate any pretentiousness. They commanded honesty.

"Hi, I'm Luke," I responded. "Do you work for Johnny?"

"No, I'm one of his daughters," she said with a laugh.

"Really," I said with a curious smile. "Well, he didn't lie."

"About what?" she asked.

"He told me that he had two beautiful girls," I answered with a smile.

"Well, thank you," she returned with a grin. "It's nice to finally meet you. Lots of dinner conversation around our house over the past few months about you."

She leaned her elbows on the top rail of the fence, cocked her head toward me, and nonchalantly asked me, "So, you beat one of Daddy's former students at the Texas Open. How is TK doing?"

I was confused by her comment. I had no idea who she was talking about.

"TK?" I questioned. "Did he play in the Texas Open?"

"Travis the Lion," she responded. "You beat him in the playoff. We were in the junior golf program together in Houston way back when. His last name is Kim, so Dad and I always called him TK. He was a little older than me, treated me like a little sister."

She looked away then back at me and said, "Then it happened."

Her voice trailed off, tears emerged in her soft eyes.

"Daddy was the best thing that ever happened to him. We had so much fun practicing and playing golf together. Dad loved him like the son he never had. TK loved Dad." She paused briefly then continued. "TK's dad was the president of a huge international oil company in Houston. Never had time for TK, so his mother just dropped him off every day at the course. They were from Korea originally. His dad was also the president of the club where Dad was pro. TK's dad played with clients, but never with TK."

"What happened?" I asked, still stunned by the revelation that Johnny was TK's first teacher.

"By the time he was 12, TK was one of the best players in the city. Dad taught him how to have fun, to be creative, to be set apart from all the other kids. Dad taught him every shot in the book, and TK could do it all," she exclaimed with pride.

"Did something change all that?" I asked, my curiosity piqued.

"My dad believed he had the perfect student to take golf to the next level. He knew TK could revolutionize the sport forever. My dad understood that it would take a revolutionary to break tradition. So he began to teach TK what he called the Pre-Set Swing. It started out as a simple drill to help people get the club in the slot at the top of their backswing. Eventually Dad and TK were convinced it was more than a drill. TK was about 13 when he implemented this technique into his game," she said. "They practiced this technique on the back of the range for a few weeks before TK used it in a tournament. The tournament was at our home course and sponsored by TK's dad's company."

"How did he do?" I asked, trying to get to the bottom of this mystery.

"He won by eight shots! It was brilliant, amazing, just unbelievable. I walked the course with my dad every step of the way," she said.

"And?" I encouraged her to continue.

"TK's dad showed up on 16. Never been to a tournament before. TK saw him and was overwhelmed that his dad would get to see him play. All the members and other parents were congratulating him on his son's fine play and thanking him for his company's sponsorship of the event. Then it happened. TK approached his ball, used the Pre-Set technique, and just blistered a ball down the fairway on the most difficult driving hole on the course."

She paused, caught her breath then continued with the shocking end to the story. "TK's dad went berserk. He grabbed my dad's arm, leading him into the woods away from the people, and began to question him about the swing. When my dad explained the brilliance of it and that TK was destined to change the game, TK's dad began to scream obscenities at my dad. His face was beat red and the veins were popping out of his neck and forehead. He put his finger in my dad's chest and insulted him in every manner possible. TK and I watched in horror over our shoulders as we walked toward his ball."

"Oh, my," I gasped.

"He questioned my dad's integrity and sanity for teaching his kid to break the traditions of this great game. He yelled at him for embarrassing him in front of the members. He berated him for embarrassing his son by teaching him to play in that manner—and to do it at their home course in a tournament he sponsored. He then promised my dad that he would do everything in his power to fire him immediately for his lapse in judgment."

I was stunned at this story.

"It doesn't end there," she said as she dropped her arms from the fence. "He then walked briskly toward TK, gesturing to his son to wait. He walked right up to him and stole his son's heart. He forbid him from seeing Johnny and told him if he ever swung that way again, it would be the last swing he would ever make."

"What did TK do?" I asked.

"The shock and fear caused him to go numb," she said with a distant stare, "He finished the final holes using a traditional swing, somehow paring in. It was a history-making victory. He shattered the course and tournament record, beating the kids even in the senior high division. Because his dad's company sponsored the event, his dad told the VP who was to award the trophy to stand aside. TK's dad gave the trophy to his son, congratulated him, then approached the mic and apologized for TK's embarrassment to the traditions of the game and assured the spectators that it wouldn't happen again."

"Oh, my," I said again.

"Then TK's dad whisked him away in his gold Mercedes. I never spoke to either of them again."

"Why not?" I asked.

"TK's dad took him down the street to a new golf-instruction facility where they emphasized the classical swing using hitting bays with no less than three camera angles, ball launch monitors, the latest in teaching tools and gadgets," she said as her voice began to rise.

"They emphasized perfection in every element of the swing, with no room for creativity and imagination. They fit him for new clubs with the latest technology. They put him in a prison of perfection, angles, vectors, and velocity. They stole the joy my dad had instilled. He became the robot prototype and poster child for the tech swing in golf. His coaches seldom let him play, relying instead on the rote hitting of balls so monitors could measure his progress with endless graphs and printouts."

"What happened to Johnny?" I led her on.

"TK's dad was powerful and manipulative. He convinced the board that it would be best to remove Dad from instruction, that he was too old school for the changing game. He convinced the board that dad was holding back the talent of the next generation. Within a few days they took instruction from him and told him to focus on the pro shop, member services, and tournament management," she explained. "Then, to rub salt into the wound, TK's dad used his weight to bring in the outfit from down the street to our range, putting them in charge of all instruction."

"And your dad's response?" I asked.

"He stood tall and smiled on the outside through it all. The members loved him, and many left because of the situation. Many also called him to meet them at a local public range for help with their games. He had to go off-site during his off hours to help his students."

She paused, kicked some dirt, then looked at me. "On the inside he was devastated. He lived to teach. He knew he was on to something with his new method. But most of all he loved TK and knew exactly what the outcome would be. He predicted that TK would be a world-beater, but that he would lose his heart, become cold and numb to victory and good play. He knew that TK would lose his joy for the game, that he would became a prisoner of technology and tradition and a pawn of his father."

"Is that when he decided to become a rancher?" I asked with curiosity.

"Yes. Within a year we drove out here on a trek for a new life, a new beginning. He knew that my sister and I loved the country and dreamed of riding and owning horses one day. He had always wanted a ranch; he dreamed of it as a boy. So here we are, ten years down the road."

She paused, wiped her moist eyes and looked all around with a big smile. She continued by paraphrasing some Old Testament scriptures, "God redeems all. He restores the land the locust destroyed, and he restores the dreams of his children."

"Dad had a great job at the club in Houston and invested well. So we were blessed with the opportunity to leave it all behind and start over in Utopia. Now he teaches golf to the locals at his course and runs cattle and horses. I work with Dad to bring freedom to abused and abandoned rescued horses, wild mustangs, and we transform retired rodeo bronc horses to carry children. Our family rodeos on the weekends most of the year. My younger sister, Faith, and I run barrels and are learning to team rope with Dad. And Mom just loves people wherever she is," she explained.

"I also sing a little, mostly to horses," she said with a laugh, knowing I had heard her. "Faith and Mom also travel for a few weeks each summer, seeking to fulfill their other dreams with dance, music, and art. They're on a short trip right now, should be back Wednesday, then they head out for another dance competition over the weekend. And we do all of this from this place called Utopia."

The sunrise was glorious this morning. A sweet breeze was blowing. The smell of fresh-cut hay filled the air, and my senses were on overload from the conversation and the beauty of Grace.

"And what about you?" she asked, "Are you willing?"

"Willing for what?" I questioned.

As she walked away, she looked over her shoulder, her golden hair drifting in the cool morning breeze and spoke these penetrating words, "To change the way the game is played."

Chapter 6

I felt the touch of a hand upon my shoulder and heard a familiar voice that gently said, "Isn't that a beautiful creature?"

"Yes, she is," I replied.

Johnny laughed and said, "No, I mean the stallion!"

We both laughed out loud, mine more out of embarrassment. He then changed the subject.

"Let's take a ride. You good with a horse?" Johnny asked.

I had grown up in Texas, so I had been riding a lot, mostly trails. But I wouldn't dare tell a horseman that I was good with a horse.

"I love to ride but have a lot to learn," I said.

"Riding a horse is a lot like going on a date. The horse can sense your emotions and read your mail. If they catch wind of fear, you could be in for a long ride," he said with warning. "Confidence is king with a horse. And, I should add, it helps on a date as well."

We both chuckled. Out of the barn came Grace, leading two horses saddled and ready to ride. Curiously, each horse had a red bandanna tied around its left front leg. I didn't ask why for fear of sounding stupid. One was a spirited paint that pranced at the site of Johnny, his master and friend. The other was a poised and graceful sorrel quarter horse that was already locked in on me, sizing up where I lay on the spectrum of greenhorn to cowboy. While my stare was a poker face of confidence, he was already analyzing my heart—and it was a few beats high.

Johnny climbed up on his horse, introducing me to Picasso as he did. I grinned at the name and started to mount my horse on the wrong side when Grace gently asked me to mount Sky from the left. She did it with a sweet and encouraging spirit, seeming to want this experience to be special for me and everyone else who ever got on a horse.

"Sky," I responded. "That's a nice name."

"Yeah, a good name for him," Grace agreed with a grin. "He used to be a bucking horse in the rodeo. Bucked so high, the rodeo cowboys named him Sky! He was legendary in the day. Very few got an eight-count on him."

She and the horse could sense my confidence waning. I was sure that horse snickered as she grabbed his face and patted his head.

"Sky was the first bronc horse dad and I trained. He hurt too many cowboys, so they banned him from the rodeo. Daddy picked him up for a steal."

The acronym TMI came to my mind as I grabbed the reigns.

"Off to Obra Maestra," Johnny announced to Grace, who smiled a big smile at the sound of that.

We took off to the west with the fragrance of summer's coronation enveloping our senses and the sun warm on our backs. My curiosity was competing with the moment. I wanted to hear about TK from Johnny's lips, but I could tell the time just wasn't right. It was time to take it all in: to hear the Pentecostal mocking bird speaking in tongues; to see the white head of a soaring Caracara hunting yet another day; to feel the power of the harnessed equine beneath this saddle, tail swishing, grasshoppers cascading, and the rhythm of it all massaging my soul. The U.S. Open was less than two weeks away, and here I was on a notorious bronc horse following a cowboy down a narrow trail in Utopia. I follow because I trust this man. Once again, I see, feel, and trust.

We crossed a creek at the bottom of a header, allowing the horses to steal a drink.

"Did you get your two gifts by sunset yesterday?" Johnny asked as he leaned back in the saddle to steady himself while the horse drank.

"Not sure," I said, thinking back to the amazing practice session.

"Think about it. Did you leave with something new in your game that you didn't have before?" he questioned, pressing me to think beyond the norm.

"My accuracy increased. I mean dramatically. So I'll count that as one." I responded.

"That's one," he agreed, with a nod of approval. "And the other?"

"The four-count process sure put a hedge around my rhythm. It was quiet a sensation. Can I count that as the second gift?" I asked.

"Well, that depends upon how important that is to you," he returned.

"You did say the key to performing great at the U.S. Open is accuracy and staying in rhythm under the intense pressure of a major," I reminded him.

"Well, my goodness. It's true that you can lead a stallion to water and make him drink," he chuckled just as Sky had his fill of water.

"Mark my words, Son," he continued with conviction. "Come game day at the U.S. Open, you will put those two gifts ahead of any Christmas package found under the tree."

Just then a bolt of adrenaline shook my peace, causing psychedelic flash cards of the U.S. Open nightmare to ricochet through my mind. I became restless in the saddle, unknowingly clutching the reins jerkily, causing Sky to shake his head and stamp the ground wildly. Sensing the undercurrent of fear that was attempting to hitch a ride with me, Johnny had me take pressure off the reins while he patted the neck of my horse. His calming presence settled over me and the horse in this juxtaposition of life: An internal thought storm enveloped by a canyon of extraordinary peace where springs meandered freely over moss-covered rocks, competing only with Newton's discovery and the seasons of life.

"Son," he whispered just above the trickling of the springs, "the battle has begun. But remember, it is not your battle. See His face, feel His presence, trust His love."

These life-giving words arrested the chaos-driven adrenalin, sending fear to search for a new victim. My breath once again went deep, and peace settled over me.

"You good?" he asked.

I nodded with confidence.

He made a clicking sound, giving a slight squeeze to Picasso, and off we went. My horse instinctively followed as we headed up a switchback toward a high plateau. The switchback was heavily shaded by the red oaks that are fond of the canyons of Utopia. The smooth red bark of the rare madrone peeks from behind the mountain laurel as if playing hide-and-seek. We broke from the header and traversed the level plateau covered in pinkish boulders, scrub oaks, and cacti for about half an hour. A break in the trees gave way to an open shelf of limestone leading to the precipice. Our horses moved cautiously toward the steep drop-off, their shoes on rock producing the familiar clip-clop sound of an old drive-in western. In awe and silence, we stopped at the entrance to a chapel without walls, where worship of the earth's creator is spontaneous.

The breeze rustled the horses' manes in this rarified view of the Texas Hill Country. There is a plethora of low-hanging fruit for the western artist in these hills. We were on top of the world in Uvalde County, overlooking the Sabinal Valley. The spring-fed waters of the Sabinal River meandered 500 feet below with elegance and grace, sensing its destiny as the giver of life in these parts.

The distinct sound of saddle leather creaked as Johnny placed both hands on the horn, stretching his legs against the stirrups, his eyes surveying the gift before us. "Obra Maestra," he whispered, as if speaking through tears. "That means masterpiece in Spanish. It's your third gift."

"It is at that," I whispered, not wanting to interrupt the sounds of life.

Johnny continued, "Each time I come up here the painting is different, yet exquisite. I love that God refreshes his art each day. I love that He does that with me as well."

"Thanks again," I said with sincerity, "for the gift you gave me Easter morning in the cemetery."

He nodded with understanding and humility. We both took it in for a few minutes.

He then looked to me as if to unload the weight of a guilty conscience. "I almost missed it."

"What?" I asked.

"This," he motioned toward the horizon. "It's easy to miss our destiny, the testimony God is painting on the canvas of our lives. We are tempted to live only the shadow of what is meant to be. I almost missed it. I had my plan, my dreams. I had life all figured out. Two kids, a beautiful wife, rose to the top of my profession to become a top-100 teacher. Earned the position of Director of Golf at a fine country club in Houston, taught golf, played sectional events and a few Tour events, coached Little League, taught Sunday School at a popular church, and lived in a nice house in a big city with lots to do and see."

"The American dream," I agreed.

"Yeah, that's what I thought. That's where I was willing to settle. Compared to this, it ain't nothin' but a stick-figure drawing," he said.

We sat in silence. Because of the incessant noise of the world, moments of silence cause most folks to believe they are missing something. Hanging out with Johnny taught me differently.

After a moment he said, "You know what I have learned?"

"What's that?" I asked.

"Many of art's greatest masterpieces were born of pain. It's the same with life. When we are in the midst of the pain, we can't perceive the first few precious strokes of the Master's hand. For me it was the loss of TK," he said, as if he could read my mind. "I heard Grace mention his name to you. Did she tell you the entire story?"

"Yes, I think so," I replied.

"I didn't tell you about him on the first visit because it wasn't time. You had enough pain to deal with without me complicating the picture," he said as he climbed off his horse. "Jump on down. Let's give the horses a rest."

We tied the horses to a tree, and they grazed the sparse but tender grass in the shade. Before we took a seat on the cliff's ledge, Johnny pulled an ice-filled Thermos of sweet tea from his saddle bag, along with a couple of old, dented tin cups. He poured the tea and offered a toast to the journey. He pushed up the front of his cowboy hat and leaned back on his elbow.

"You see, I thought TK was the one who would revolutionize the golf swing. He was young, free, and unencumbered. He was in love with the game, open to innovation and creativity. There wasn't anything he couldn't do. I thought he would be the one to introduce the Pre-Set method to the world. I thought he would be part of the masterpiece being written through my life," Johnny stopped for a moment to take a sip from his cup.

"The Artist had other plans, a different painting in mind. At that time my life looked as though it was shattered. I loved that boy. I can't tell you what it was like watching his tear-filled eyes peering out of the back window as his dad drove him away. But the Artist was in full control. Thus you and I are sitting here today, both having experienced deep pain followed by a rebirth, and the power and freedom that comes with it."

He stopped for a moment as a rush of wind came upon us. It seemed to be from a heavenly source, giving weight to Johnny's words. The wildness of the moment caused me to shiver, though it wasn't cold. My spirit was entering the Obra Maestra, completely saturated by the colors of a divine encounter. The wind spoke of greatness, and I listened as Johnny went deeper still.

"When you showed up in April, dragging the anvil of a monumental meltdown, I sensed the movement of the paintbrush in your life. While you couldn't see it, I was given clarity on your behalf," Johnny said as he artfully added an illustration from the ancient scriptures: "Samuel anointed David as the next king when he was a naive shepherd boy. But it wasn't until later that a guy named Jonathan saw with clarity the divine greatness and called it out of David in the midst of David's painful and perilous rise to kingship."

I couldn't help but notice the name of Jonathan. I shivered a second time at the thought that life's Artist considered me worthy of a Johnny as well. We sat quietly for a while, contemplating the moment. I listened for the whisper of heaven as I leaned into the Obra Maestra. The wind settled as the distinct call of a red-tail hawk shrieked across the expanse, soaring high into the face of the wind.

"Fear," Johnny whispered as his eyes followed the flight of the majestic hawk towering above the valley. "Fear is the opponent. It keeps the common man from soaring. The fear of broken dreams, failed attempts, unfulfilled expectations. Fear of missing out, being lied to, being invalidated. Fear of being insignificant, not measuring up, being left out and unlovable. Fear of being found out and the shame and guilt of the consequences of wrong decisions. Fear of what we believe others think about us. Fear is insidious."

"When I bring in a new horse, it doesn't need to be broken. I have one purpose: to bring freedom from its fear," He looked over at Picasso and nodded. "That horse was scared of its shadow when we got him from a rescue center. He is fearless now. He can run barrels, team rope, or carry kids. Freedom is a powerful force."

"Another author-mentor to me was one of Jesus' closest friends. Another guy named John. John tells us in one of his short books that perfect love casts out all fear. He defined God as love. When we put those two together we get this: God casts out all fear. When you see His face, feel His presence, and trust His love, SFT, there is no room for fear. Son, sport psychology can't do that.

"Yesterday's lesson was about fear at its core. You just might change the way golf is played," Johnny locked in on me with those compassionate yet piercing eyes. "I thought it was going to be TK, but the Artist disagreed. He has anointed you. And the U.S. Open is your debut."

"The Utopia Pre-Set will be a part of the future of golf, and the U.S. Open is its unveiling. If you fear, you will fail and be laughed off the Tour. If you embrace the challenge, realize the call, and play with the passion and focus of a revolutionary, you will be trailblazing a new method for all who play the game this day forward."

"That's a lot of weight to carry," I said.

"That's fear speaking to you. I think there is something bigger than a golf swing going on. Always is when the Artist speaks. It is His weight to carry. You've been invited to cross the line first. I believe there will be a moment of confirmation in your spirit this week. Be patient and be listening, it may come in a whisper or a roar, but it will come. And ..." He paused to pour us another drink.

"And?" I asked, urging him on.

"And you will be attacked by some for daring to break tradition. It will be bloody," Johnny said. "But when you take a stand and deliver, and when you respond in love to the scapegoats of the dream-thief, the blood won't be yours in the end, it will be the blood of false tradition that is left in the wake of freedom. Perfect love casts out all fear."

I was both humbled and honored at his words. He saw things in me that I couldn't or wouldn't have dared to see or dream. We spoke very few more words that afternoon. Conversation can get in the way of defining moments.

And so we shared sweet tea at the edge of heaven and listened to the melodies of real life as we gazed at the ever-changing Obra Maestra.

Chapter 7

Day four was solo day, as Johnny called it. He exhorted me to go to the course, spend the day exploring the new technique. Get used to scoring using it. Hit different shots, test out the method with the wind, against the wind, low shots, high shots, and everything in between. Especially work with the short wedges, gaining the feel for half and three-quarter shots. Finish by playing nine holes with one ball for score.

When I went to the course and began to play and keep score, I finally got it. It clicked. I understood the depth and genius inherent in this teaching. Johnny wasn't just smart like a fox, he was an extraordinary thinker and inventor. What Johnny had seen went beyond normal instruction. It was the most comprehensive yet simple idea. It resonated deep in my golfing soul. What Johnny had taught me was a swing and process that intricately and brilliantly combined the mental and physical games. This truly was a game-day breakthrough.

It was a special day of letting rather than forcing, swinging to a four-count rhythm rather than trying to hit positions. He was right: I wasn't overhauling my swing, just changing the order of two elements. I was excited to be on the cutting edge, but I was nervous to be the one unveiling this unique move in front of such a large crowd of discerning spectators at the U.S. Open.

During the day, Johnny dropped by and invited me to join him and his family at midweek church service that evening. Johnny said that he had a little part in the service and that tonight's teaching would help equip me for the U.S. Open and beyond. The anticipation of the evening piqued my curiosity and served as fuel to my day. I looked forward to finally meeting his wife and youngest daughter as well. They were expected to be home from their trip by the start of church

Following a day of practice and a chicken-fried steak dinner laden with cream gravy at the Lost Maples Cafe, I headed for the church as the sun began to set behind the hills. The service had already begun as I walked in, so I took one of the few remaining seats in the back of the room. I noticed Johnny and his family on the front row. He glanced at me across the room with a warm smile and nod. I looked forward to meeting his wife and youngest daughter later that evening. The crowded room revealed that there was something special about this place. As the music began, I understood. There was a Spirit in this out-of-the-way church on the outskirts of Utopia that transported all of us to a footstool in front of the Almighty.

Eventually the pastor walked to the front carrying a barstool. He set it strategically on the stage then moved behind the pulpit. He directed the congregation to open their Bibles to an obscure two-verse story hidden in the pages of 2nd Samuel. Those who had their Bibles, which was most of the folks, were led to chapter 23, verses 11b – 12.

He gave the crowd a few moments to find their places. He prefaced that this was a story about one of David's three mighty men. He went on to say that our dreams rest in the balance with these two verses. He had my attention as I anticipated all that was in front of me.

"…When the Philistines banded together at a place where there was a field full of lentils," the pastor started and then paused and posed a rhetorical question to his audience.

"What is a lentil?" he asked.

A few folks replied, "It's a bean."

The pastor quipped, "Yes, they were at a bean field."

He then continued the reading, "Israel's troops fled from them. But Shammah took his stand in the middle of the field. He defended it and struck the Philistines down, and the Lord brought about a great victory."

The pastor closed his Bible, took off his reading glasses, and paraphrased the passage.

"It looks like to me that the most powerful army in the world, based on the great feats that preceded this story, met up with some big guys at a bean field. It seems like they saw the size of the Philistines and determined that the bean field was not worth fighting and dying for, so they high-tailed it out of there like a bunch of losers." He paused for effect.

"But," he paused and drove home a point. "And that is a huge word in this story. But Shammah stayed and took a stand and defeated the enemy by the power of God.

"The question is, why did Shammah stay and the other guys on his team run in fear? Here's the deal, and it's a big deal to all of us today. This at its core is about God-given dreams.

"Many years earlier, God gave the Israelites a dream of the promised land through Moses. Eventually, Joshua ushered them into this land. Here we are a few years down the line, and the Israelites are willing to give away territory. They are willing to give away some of the dream. And, folks, when you start giving away the territory of your God-given dreams, you in essence are giving away a part of your heart. God says to guard your heart, for it is the wellspring of life.

"Shammah had a different perspective, a perspective we need today.

"First, Shammah knew that we live in the midst of a battle, and it is the battle between good and evil, God and the enemy of God. It's a battle for the hearts and souls of men and women and children. It's an epic battle for eternity. Unlike the other soldiers, Shammah dressed the part of a contender when he woke up. The others dressed for show; they were pretenders. They liked to be known as soldiers, but it was window-dressing on this day.

"Second, Shammah didn't see an insignificant bean field; he saw sacred ground. He believed it was part of the original dream, thus worth fighting for.

"Third, he saw the big guys, but he knew size didn't matter in God's economy. He also knew that the real battle was not against these guys, but the one who had stolen their hearts and dreams along the way. He knew that the big guys were but pawns of the enemy. And he knew in his spirit a truth that would eventually be engraved in scripture, 'He who is in me is greater than he who is in the world.'

"And then to the amazement of us all, he takes a stand in the face of insurmountable odds. The only way he could have walked into the center of that field was to know beyond a shadow of a doubt who he was. His identity wasn't about a score, possessions, talent, or wealth. His identity was embedded in God. He knew he was a child of God, and thus God would be with him. The scriptures reveal that God says, 'I will never leave nor forsake you.' They also say that 'I can do all things through Christ who strengthens me.'

"Another thing Shammah knew was that going to the middle of the field alone was not great military strategy, because it would be easy to surround him. However he understood that two plus two doesn't always equal four in God's economy. More often than not, God likes to do things that require faith over logic. With Gideon he whittled down his army from 30,000 to 300 to do battle against a huge opposition. He told Joshua, the great military leader of Israel, to take Jericho by simply walking around the city, not attacking it. He told David to take down Goliath with a sling. So Shammah went where he was told and took a stand and stared down the enemy. I also believe that Shammah knew he would win or be in heaven in about five minutes, so what was there to lose?

"Finally, the text says he defended the field, and God brought about a great victory. I can hear Shammah exhorting from heaven right now saying, 'Tell them the truth: God brought about the victory. I was just privileged to have a front-row seat as God destroyed the one who wanted to steal a piece of the dream on that day!'"

The pastor paused to let the weight of this great story sink in. He wanted it to go deep.

"God is looking for contenders for the field. The great adventure awaits all who are willing to step out in faith to save their own dreams and guard the dreams of others. Jesus said, 'The thief comes only to steal and kill and destroy; I have come that you may have life and have it to the full.' Folks, life to the full is taking a stand in the middle of a field of dreams. There are no insignificant dreams if God has authored them."

The pastor closed his Bible and put his glasses in his pocket as all the lights were turned off, with the exception of one light shining down directly on the stool. The pastor took a seat next to his wife on the front row. A silence fell over the room. After a few moments of anticipation, Johnny rose in the dark and walked to the front of the church, slowly climbed the stairs and moved his shadowy form into the light surrounding the stool. In his hand was a worn manuscript within a leather binder that he opened as he took a seat upon the stool. There was a radiance surrounding this man, not from a smile or facial expression. It was a radiance that is seen in those sent from heaven on a rescue mission to the world. It draws forth the heart and envelops the seeker with assurance and hope and anticipation.

And without any pretension or introduction he began to read a story he had written.

Chapter 8:

Guardian of Her Dreams

During the Christmas season in a quaint country village not too long ago a little girl received her dream. You see, all children have dreams. God plants a dream seed in the heart of each child. For children hear the voice of God. They hear the voice of their destiny, the voice of hope.

On Christmas Eve the little girl and her father were strolling down the rustic main street of this well-decorated, old-fashioned village when they came upon an antique shop. Though this particular antique shop was void of any visible Christmas decorations, the objects in the window piqued the imagination of the child, so they entered the shop, just as so many before them had. Antique shops, you see, hold great intrigue to young and old alike. All who enter believe somewhere deep in their heart that they just might find a hidden treasure. These two were no different.

The shop, like most antique shops, was dark and grey with a distinct musty scent that hung like smoke in the stale air. The shop was a place void of life. It was a place where used and tired-out items rested from their years of service sadly displaying their mark of honor: Do not touch.

The few patrons in the shop on this day were looking for

something, though nothing in particular. For that is how it is in the antique shop.

In the antique shop people often enter a story, a story of lost dreams. They see the items of their youth and remember a time when they, too, had a dream. But like the old and lifeless porcelain dolls with torn and tattered lace, life has passed them by. So too has their dream.

The old books remind the antiques-shopper of childhood adventures with happy endings. The aged rocking horse brings memories of bygone Christmas mornings. The creaky wooden rocker fills their heart with longing for deceased grandparents. And an old album cover sears their heart with embers of lost love.

But they keep coming back, for as long as there are memories, there is still hope that somewhere among them they will find a glimmer of the rekindled dream. It often happens when a treasure is found in an antique shop. An item passed over by so many sparks the dream in a listless soul. It is as though divine intervention interrupts life at just the right moment with just the right item, and life changes. And every so often a person emerges from the shop with a relic to many, but a seed of a rekindled dream to one. That is why antique stores intrigue so many.

As the father and his little girl entered the shop, the eyes of the antique dealer sharpened. Antique shops are "no touch" shops, and little girls presented a challenge. The hearts of all little girls are nurtured by touch.

They moved slowly through the ever-changing maze of lifeless items. Unlike a department store, there is no order to the

74

display of goods. The father watched his daughter as her eyes sparkled with the intrigue of treasures never before seen. She had many questions, for she was young and everything was so old. The patient father answered the endless stream of questions, all the while weaving in several stories of his past related to the items. This thrilled the little girl, who listened carefully to his every word. To her, he hung the moon.

In one tucked-away nook near the back of the store the little girl's heart leaped at what she saw. There, half-hidden beneath a handmade quilt, sat a miniature piano. The little girl loved music. Though she had only been taking lessons for a short while, she knew she would make beautiful music someday.

She was compelled forward and knelt in front of the one-of-a-kind instrument. To her this was indeed a priceless piece. Though the tiny piano only had fifteen keys, these were more than enough to make music. It had been years since the piano had been played. And since it was an antique, no one dared to touch the keys. How sad, the young girl thought, that an instrument meant to make music sat quiet. The father was in a nearby aisle, lost in his memories but aware that his little girl was near him.

The little girl removed the quilt and, unbeknownst to her, the "do not touch" tag as well. She stood motionless, staring with delight at the most beautiful instrument she had ever seen. Though very old, like a Stradivarius, its age had only made it more beautiful. The dedication of the craftsman was evident.

The piano was half as tall as the girl and about that wide as well. In front of the instrument was a small bench that seemed to have been made just for the little girl.

And then it happened: She received her dream. The voice of God said, "Have a seat and play. It is your music that will move the hearts of many to seek my face."

Her heart became warm. As she sat down, she was transported to a heavenly stage. Time stood still as she reached out her hands and touched the keys. The ivory felt smooth and cool to her soft little fingers. It was as though the antique shop had been transformed. A beam of light from the sun breaking through the clouds streamed through the old window panes, settling on the girl's golden hair. A discerning ear could hear the sound of a thousand angels' wings fluttering eagerly for a front-row seat. The little girl glowed in the sunlight of her dream. Carnegie Hall would be blessed to witness such a moment.

She caressed the keys, yellowed with age, wondering if they would respond. Finding middle C, she began. Since the Christmas season was upon them Silent Night coursed through her fingers, for it was a song that her little mind had retained.

The sound of music broke the silence of the library like atmosphere. It was blessed music, sounding as though it had been piped in through the velvet filters of heaven. First the father heard and then he turned and saw. In stunned awe he stood, praying that this moment would never pass. Patrons stopped their search and listened. They peeked through bookcases and peered over tables and lamps to catch a glimpse of pure joy incarnate.

Suddenly, life began to appear all around them. Dreams began to inhabit the shop. The shoppers one by one reached out and embraced revealed treasures that only moments before had seemed like ordinary, antiquated items. A revival of life was taking place in the hearts of the people. Though too focused to notice, the little girl's dream had indeed begun. Her music was changing lives.

A line began to form at the antique dealer's register, which brought him great delight and hope. He too had lost his dream a long time ago. Bitterness had replaced hope as he eked out a living in the musty old shop. He, who seldom sold more than a few items in a day, had never seen such a quick gathering in such a short amount of time. Just as he was about to collect money from the first customer, he too heard the sound.

But to him it was not the sound of heaven but the sound of alarm. He excused himself in a huff and made a dash for the source of the music. He jolted the girl from her dream with his booming voice. "Do not play the piano! Can't you read?" He reached down and picked up the "do not touch" sign from the floor taping it back to the piano. "This is a priceless antique, not an instrument!" He continued, "I knew you were trouble when I saw you enter the store. Where is your father?"

The father appeared from behind the bookshelf, stunned by the sudden appearance of the angry dealer.

"Sir," he said, "this is my daughter, and I take full responsibility for letting her play."

He reached for the little girl as the ray of sun disappeared behind a gray cloud. She buried her head into his chest in shame. She felt like a thief. And she began to sob.

As the music ceased, so did life in that little antique shop.

All the patrons looked down at their treasures, the items that only moments ago had rekindled their dreams. But all they could see now was junk. Confused by the turn of events, one by one they slipped out of line returning the objects to their former place. Just as they came in, they left the shop with no dream. They left with a heart only hope could patch.

The antique owner returned to his register, bewildered at the mass exit. His hope, too, was dashed once again, and he was angry. He glared at the father and little girl, blaming them for ruining his business and doing it on Christmas Eve. They were the last to leave. Even though it wasn't yet closing time, he locked the door quickly behind them and turned the sign from Open to Closed in the store-front window.

The father carried the sobbing little girl to a nearby park bench. He held her close to his chest like a shepherd holds a lamb. He stroked her hair and gently rocked her back and forth as he prayed that God would protect him from the rage he felt in his heart toward the antique dealer. He was born to be a warrior, a protector of his flock. But long ago God had taught him that seldom was the visible battle the true battle.

Like all fathers, he was called to be the guardian of his child's dreams, and that was exactly what he was to do. In his own flesh he wanted to fight a man, but the wisdom of God showed him the true enemy. It was time for the girl to receive the truth, for the father knew that the truth would set her free.

So he dried her weary eyes and brushed the tear-stained hair from her face. He loved her cheeks most of all. He sat her on his lap and asked if he might have a "cheek snack," a secret code between the two of them for a kiss. It brought a smile to her face as he gently kissed her cheek, saying the salty ones were the best.

Then he began the lesson of a lifetime. He told her that God was a dream-giver and that it was evident that He had visited her in the shop today. But, he also said, there was a dream-taker as well. He was a thief, and he wanted to kill, steal, and destroy all dreams. There was a fierce battle between good and evil and we live in the midst of it. Most people don't realize it; therefore they give away their dream without a fight. When you give away your dream, you give away your heart, the wellspring of life.

The good news is that those who know the dream-giver have the power to overcome the evil thief. But they must hold onto their dream or they will lose this power. All real dreams lead to God, and that is why the enemy wants to take them away. Once people give up their God-given dream, they substitute others. But these others never fulfill. They are false dreams, empty dreams. That is where most people live: prisoners of the dream-taker.

The little girl asked if the antique dealer was the dream-taker. The father said that at first glance you would think so. Without discernment from God, we would enter the wrong battle, as so many do. We would want to fight the antique dealer. You see, the dream-taker uses the prisoners of lost dreams as his scapegoat. But the true enemy is the dream-taker himself. That is where God's power comes into play. He gives eyes of discernment and hearts of restraint to those who seek Him so that they enter the right battle, the battle for eternity.

The father and little girl looked back toward the shop. The enemy took the antique dealer's dream many years ago, leaving him empty and bitter. Now the enemy uses him to help in the war against dreams. The sad thing for him and all other prisoners is that they don't even know they are being used.

The dream-taker is like God in the sense that you cannot always see him; he is a spirit. The good news is that the dream-giver is more powerful, and for those who know God, the dream-taker has no power to steal their dream.

"Did he steal my dream, Papa?" the little girl asked. "I feel so ashamed about playing the piano that I don't ever want to play again."

The father looked into his daughter's eyes and said, "That choice is yours. God himself has given you your dream. You can give it to the dream-taker or keep it for yourself. It is up to you."

"I want to keep it," she said. "But how?"

The father reached for her hand and held it tightly. "You must fight for it and a dream from God is worth fighting for. You must become a little warrior, and the time to start is now," he emphasized.

"But I am only a little girl," she said sheepishly.

The father asked her to look into his eyes. And with the conviction of God himself he said, "It is God's battle, not yours. So do not fear."

The father asked her a question. "Tell me your dream. What did God say to you today?"

Remembering back to that divine moment she replied, "He

said that I will make music that will cause people to seek God."

The father's eyes welled up with tears of joy as he responded, "I have known in my spirit from the day you were conceived that you were destined to serve God. What a beautiful dream. Your music will minister to people and lead them toward God. What a wonderful dream."

He was quiet for a moment, sensing the voice of God speaking to his heart. So he listened.

"The battle has begun," he heard God say to his heart, "Take her back into the shop. She is a worthy little warrior with my strength. Tell her and lead her; you are the guardian of her dream. Return to the shop and tell the antique dealer you want to buy the piano. But tell him you will buy it only if he allows your little girl to play one song first. Tell him you will pay twice the asking price if the piano makes music and all the keys work. If some of the keys don't work, you will pay the asking price and take it anyway. If you do what I ask, both of you will see a portion of your dream come true this Christmas Eve. Trust me, and I will bless you."

The father contemplated deeply what he heard. "Where would the money come from? What if the antique dealer is too angry? What if my daughter is too afraid?" he thought, as the battle in his mind escalated. The father knew that this was always the enemy's ploy, planting doubt where God demanded faith. He had been in too many battles to accept the enemy's plan on this occasion.

He stood and lifted the little girl up so that she stood on the park bench, looking him in the eye. He then asked, "Are you ready to make your dream come true?"

"How?" she asked naively.

The father told the little girl what God had just put in his heart. "We must enter the unseen battle and face our opponent. We must do something that isn't easy or comfortable. We must return to the shop, buy the piano, and you must play a song."

"But won't he yell at me again?" she feared.

"No," he said patiently, "because we will own the piano."

"But, Papa, isn't the piano too expensive? We don't have much money," she said with great concern.

With firm conviction the father answered, "We must do what God has instructed. He said, Trust me and I will bless you this Christmas Eve."

The father grabbed both of the little girl's cold hands and said, "Let's pray first." The girl was glad, for praying would buy more time.

They bowed their heads right there on the street, oblivious to the scurrying Christmas shoppers around them.

The father prayed, "Dear Father in heaven, we have no power to defeat the enemy, but you do. Thank you for going before us and parting the sea. Give us courage to go arm in arm and do battle together, father and daughter. Let my little girl know of your great love, protection, and strength this day. Let her know that though she is weak, you are strong, and that though she is little, you are big. Let her know that you have called her to be a little warrior this day. Surround us with your angels and let us be part of a great miracle this

Christmas Eve. Amen."

He held her hand as she jumped from the bench, and they moved toward the closed door of the shop. By now, the shop-keeper had pulled all the curtains. As they approached the door, the little girl hid behind her papa's leg. She hung on to his pant leg with her trembling little fingers. The father rapped his knuckles on the door with the authority of a man on a mission. There was no response, so he knocked again, this time with even more authority.

The curtains parted, and the door opened with a jerk. The foreboding bearded antique dealer glared in disgust as he stood toe to toe with the father. He reeked of alcohol and cigarette smoke, revealing his solution to the great disappointment he had experienced.

"What do you want, to steal more business?" he roared. "Haven't you and your unruly girl caused enough harm for one day?"

"Sir," the father said in a voice that could calm the sea. "I would like to make an offer on the piano if it is still for sale."

The dealer took a step back and quickly began to backpedal, knowing that a sale of this magnitude would make his day.

"Well, well," he said, clearing his throat. "Come in, and let's discuss this."

As the father and girl entered, the dealer turned over the closed sign and opened the curtains, letting in light to the dimly lit shop.

The father continued, "I want to make a deal with you."

This thrilled the dealer, because he was the master of taking advantage of greenhorn antique shoppers like the father and little girl.

"Here is my proposition," the father started. "If you will let my little girl play a song on the piano, and if all the piano keys work and make music, I will pay you double its price. If it is broken and some of the keys don't make music, I will still buy it at full price."

The dealer couldn't believe his ears. It was a better deal than he could have devised.

The dealer replied quickly, "Why sure. That will be fine. Let's go find that piano."

As they walked back toward the instrument, warmth came over the girl's fearful heart. It was the same feeling she'd had earlier in the day as her dream was given to her. The sprouted seed was still alive.

They rounded the bookshelf, and there sat the piano, with the quilt draped over it along with the "do not touch" sign. The dealer quickly removed the quilt. He had cranked open the window near the piano to let the cigarette smoke escape. They could hear the sound of footsteps along Main Street just outside the window.

The father nudged the girl forward. Though anxious, the warmth in her heart grew at the sight of her new piano, the most beautiful Christmas present she had ever seen. She sat down as the sun once again broke through the cloud and envel-

oped her with a radiance never seen by the dealer.

He backed up, feeling the supernatural presence that began to fill the nook. His heart was in his throat as the little girl placed her fingers upon the ivory as though they were meant to be there. She began to play the Christmas carol, transforming the shop into a heavenly music hall once again. This time, though, the dealer fell to his knees, held up only by the strength of the invisible angels all around. Something so profound was happening in his heart that he began to weep quietly.

The music carried out the open window, spilling out on the passersby. Many were intrigued and entered the undecorated shop, seeking to catch a glimpse of the source of the music that had tapped into their souls.

The dealer staggered to his feet, wiping his moist eyes. He motioned to the father that he would be right back. He disappeared momentarily into a storage room and returned, holding an ancient violin case. He knelt next to the little girl who, consumed by the moment, was unaware of his presence. He opened the battered case on the rough pine floor, revealing a dusty violin that looked as if it had not been played in years.

The dealer pulled out the old violin and bow. He blew off the dust and nuzzled the instrument next to his beard. As his bow arm rose with the bow gently held in the fingers of his calloused hand, he closed his eyes as if he were about to receive his first kiss. The bow touched the strings for the first time in years. Without taking the time to tune the instrument for fear of missing the moment, he began to play. Oh, how majestically he played! The sound of the piano and violin merged in the air, creating a dance of joy.

At once the store was filled with life. The miracle was back, and the old objects of ancient days once again began to represent lost dreams. People by the dozens picked up items, finding their lost dreams.

A young single lady who had been hurt by love found her dream in an old high chair. She had always dreamed of having a house full of children but had given up hope that she would ever get married. She was ready to look for a husband again.

A wayward teenager found his dream in a worn-out army uniform. Years ago he had dreamed of serving his country and becoming a hero. But he had lost his dream in the meaningless meanderings of life.

A housewife whose children had all grown found her dream in a tattered grammar book. She had dreamed of teaching children to read but an early pregnancy forced her to leave college early. It was time to finish what she had started so many years ago.

A doctor found his dream in the form of an early-century doctor's bag. He had dreamed of serving Third World countries, but the stress of work and his preoccupation with climbing the ladder in his profession had occupied his mind for years. Now he was ready to enter the short-term mission field, antiquated doctor's bag in tow.

An old man saw old fishing lures and remembered his dream of following in his grandfather's footsteps, teaching his grandchildren to fish. Fishing was always a means for passing down wisdom to the next generation.

An older couple who had met at camp many years ago

dreamed of one day starting a youth camp. But once married, they fell in love with work and drifted apart from each other and their dream. It was the look and smell of the old kerosene lantern that returned their senses to the camp and their dream. The thought of serving together in a common cause lit the fire of their love. They found their place in the long line, now curling through the aisles of the shop.

The dealer was unaware of the line because he too had found his lost dream. When he was a child, God told him one day that he would make music that would bring people great joy. But whenever an antique instruments arrived at the shop his father forbid him to play them for fear that they might break and lose their value. His father would not spend money on a new instrument because they were poor. A middle school teacher inspired him and taught him to play the violin. The teacher told him that he had a special gift for music. But the father said it was a waste of time and there was no money to be made playing a violin. The dealer had spent years in the prison of bitterness because his own father had been used by the dream-taker to steal his God-given dream.

The people in line didn't seem to mind the wait as they began to sing along with the heavenly chorus to "Silent Night." Finally the little girl stopped her playing and looked up at the dealer in awe. He put down his bow and opened his eyes. They twinkled as they looked at the little girl as if she had just saved his life.

The dealer then noticed the line. With great apology but hope in his heart, he quickly moved to the register. He had never seen such a line nor sold so many items in a day. The people were all happy to wait and thanked him over and over for the music and the treasures. Finally, the last two in line approached the register. It was the father and little girl. The father was holding the miniature piano.

The dealer moved from behind the counter and embraced the man, asking for forgiveness for his earlier behavior. He knelt down and looked the little girl in the eye and said, "This is your piano. It has always been yours. I have just been holding it for you. There will be no charge. Merry Christmas."

She gave him a hug around the neck, the first in his life from a child. His heart melted.

As the father and his daughter walked out of the shop on that Christmas Eve, the little girl said, "Papa, what is your dream?"

"I was riding a pony as a young boy when I received my dream. God told me that I would be a rescuer. I would spend my life riding in on a great white imaginary horse, rescuing those trapped in the prison of lost dreams." He looked down at her as she thought deeply of what he said.

Then she asked, "Like the antique dealer?"

"Yes," he replied.

She smiled a big smile and said, "Like me?"

"Yes," he repeated.

As the sunset glowed all around them, tears began to roll down his cheeks. His daughter thanked him for rescuing her and asked if she could have a cheek snack. He knelt down and she kissed him on the cheek. Then hugged his neck as if she'd never let go and whispered in his ear, "I like the salty ones the best."

God delivered his promise to them that Christmas Eve.

From that day and forever more the little girl lived her dream.

The antique dealer played his music in the shop every day. He removed the "do not touch" signs from the musical instruments and all the other items. He encouraged every child who walked through the door to try out the instruments. He never again saw himself as an antique dealer. He knew he was in the business of helping others find lost dreams. His business thrived more than it ever had. And he lived his dream, bringing joy to many. He fell deeply in love with the lady that bought the high chair. They eventually married and had many children together.

From that year on, the antique shop was the most decorated building in the village at Christmas time. And it was said that the village Santa Claus looked a lot like the antique dealer.

The End.

As Johnny closed the yellowed manuscript, the light shining down on him faded as a new light shone down on the small piano from the story that rested on a different part of the stage. The congregation gasped, and a murmur could be heard throughout the crowd.

Johnny's youngest daughter Faith appeared out of the shadows. She knelt in front of the worn keys of this ancient little instrument. She placed her hands upon the keys and began to play "Silent Night," just as she had many years ago in the old antique store. Though she had grown and the instrument remained the same, the two were etched as one in the annals of eternity.

Faith watched her promised dream unfold as men, one by one, spontaneously began to move to the front of the room and kneel near the stage. Dim lights replaced the darkness throughout the room. Before long most every man in attendance was on his knees, weeping for lost territory or "do not touch" signs he had placed on the dreams of his children.

Sensing the overwhelming grief, the pastor stepped into the light as Faith continued to play, tears of joy streaming down her cheeks. The pastor's wisdom assured all of us that there was a God of grace that specialized in resurrecting dreams and lives, for that is the message of the cross, the message of grace. He quoted the Apostle Paul, saying, "Therefore if anyone is in Christ, he is a new creation; the old has gone, the new has come." He then reached out his hands and prayed over all of us. He prayed fervently that on this night we would leave this altar of resurrected dreams, as he called it, with the assurance of grace and the resolve of Shammah. That in the power and leading of the Almighty we would claim the fields in front of us, reclaim lost territory, and that we would endeavor to guard the God-given dreams of our children and friends.

And with that the women and children joined their men and prayed over them as freedom began to reign. Guilt melted away in the face of grace. Honor and resolve replaced shame, and the flickering light of hope became a blaze as men stood with new life.

The moment was too profound for words; the normal after-service banter was replaced with awe and wonder as folks quietly exited. "Silent Night" drifted into the parking lot, rising up to the heavens, causing the stars to applaud with their twinkling lights on this early summer evening. And on this night everyone knew they had encountered the Dream-Giver in a small church on the outskirts of Utopia.

● Johnny's U.S. Open ●

Chapter 9

On day five I did what I always did when I couldn't sleep. I began hitting balls at sun-up. My lungs feasted on the fresh, morning air of the Sabinal Valley. The dew beads shimmered like a field full of diamonds as the sun crept over the eastern hills. The range is a golfer's haven. It's our go-to place to think, ponder, and figure things out. Last night's magnum opus coursed through my imagination, inspiring thoughts of greatness for the first time in my life. To defend a field of dreams awoke the Shammah in me. But what dreams? What I really needed was a visit from the Dream-Giver, which Johnny believed would happen this week. So I prayed between shots for an encounter.

I had dreamed of winning the U.S. Open, but it wasn't *the* dream. I was beginning to understand that victories in the games of life were only a destination along the way to something much bigger. I also knew that the new swing was somehow a vehicle, not an end unto itself.

At about eight Johnny showed up at the range in his vintage Ford pickup, slung open the door, and said, "Come on, let's go for a ride. You'll have plenty of time to practice more this afternoon." Somehow he sensed my spirit and knew that last night was a door-opening experience. Today was about walking through the door.

We drove deep into his ranch to a 25-acre oat patch. Leaving the truck at the gate, we hiked to the middle of the cool, green field of oats dotted with encroaching wildflowers. It was one of the few planting fields on the large ranch. Standing in the middle of the field provided a 360-degree panorama of the Texas Hills. This piece of sacred sustenance-producing ground was surrounded by 10 different oak-covered peaks. The field itself was flat and showed evidence of the many and varied animals that tracked through this restaurant of choice during the winter and spring.

He put his foot up on a large, white stone, pointing out that he often sat on this stone to watch the sun rise and to speak with God. He said that this field reminded him of the lentil field that called Shammah to greatness. Chiseled into the stone was the number 33:3. Johnny shared that it was the verse written by one of his favorite Old Testament authors and mentors, Jeremiah. He explained that in that verse God literally says to call to Him, and He will answer and tell you deep and unsearchable things, things you do not know. Johnny added that either God is for real and speaks as His word says, or it's all a lie. He went on to say how much his life changed when he started taking God at His word. He said it all started right here on this rock.

"It's out here, away from the distractions of the rat race, where I hear most clearly. It's a place where I catch a glimpse of the supernatural settling upon the natural, revealing parables of life. Let me show you what I mean," Johnny said.

"Best we can tell this field has been plowed and planted in oats for nearly a hundred years. There is no telling how many different plows and planters have been used, but let me show you one of them, the one that brought me to my knees a few years back."

We continued our walk to the opposite side of the field where Johnny opened a double gate used by the ranchers of years gone by to access the field with their tractors and plows. We walked down the fence line to an antique farm implement sitting among an encroaching persimmon bush, along with cactus and a busy red ant bed.

"Some ol' rancher pulled this plow and seed bin out of the field for the last time, unhooked it, and left it here, never to do again what it was made to do," Johnny said in almost a sacred tone. "This happened about 70 years ago."

Johnny explained that he had walked near this area before but never really noticed the old plow and seed bin until one day after an enriching time in the field. He said that time spent with God always intensifies his senses and he becomes a noticer, code for being sensitive to parables unfolding around us.

He continued, "On this particular day, as I was closing the gate I noticed this antique and was intrigued. As I walked over, I became curious about how it worked. I saw the plow and then this seed bin."

He asked me to take a look inside. As I lifted the lid, frozen by the rust of hopelessness, it creaked and groaned, as if protecting some entombed treasure. The light rays from the sun invaded the darkness of the bin, revealing that indeed there was treasure: It was half full of seed, seed meant to be planted 70 years ago, stuck in the seed bin never to produce fruit.

At that moment I understood that parables like the one Johnny shared last night exist and that talking with God creates 33:3 moments that transform insight. I could tell that Johnny's spirit was still moved by the sight of his discovery.

"Dream seed," Johnny whispered. "I believe that God plants dreams in the hearts of all men, but for most of us, the seed gets trapped inside. Mostly it's fear that traps them—fear that it's too big, that I am too small, that I might fail, that I might be laughed at, that the cost is too great."

Johnny dodged an assault from an insidious red wasp that furiously flew from his guard post in a dark corner of the bin, a prophetic sign of Johnny's next comment.

"And the source of the fear is the accuser of man, the dream-taker. You heard about him last night at church," he said. "My friend, he is the true enemy of the dream seed."

Carefully looking for other wasps, I reached in to feel the seed. I grasped a handful allowing it to run through my fingers and fall back into the bin. I kept one seed in my hand, holding it between my thumb and index finger. I felt remorse and heartache for the inanimate object, as if it were begging to be planted.

"Keep it," I heard Johnny say.

"Here's a water bottle. Take your journal and the seed and find an oak to sit under. I think God wants to talk with you about that seed, to identify it for you today and speak to you about it. It's time to plant it, to free it from fear. See if you can't identify the dream seed God has given you as well as the fears that prevented it from being planted. Write in your journal all you hear from the Dream-Giver and plant the seed in the oat patch as a symbol to Him that you will trust Him with your dream. The Bible says, 'Unless a seed falls to the ground and dies, it cannot produce fruit.' We have to give it to Him to see it fulfilled."

Johnny went on to say that a farmer had told him one oat plant could produce 10 or more seed heads easily. Johnny shared that he had done the math and that if one of the seeds in the seed bin had been planted 10 years ago and produced 10 seeds, and each of those had produced 10 the next year, and if this continued for 10 years, that one seed would have produced 10 billion seeds.

"The seed you hold in your hand represents the power of the

dream seed inside of you to change history, to change eternity," Johnny said in earnest.

"On your last trip you buried the lies that had been holding you back in life. This time you are planting seed that will propel you into true greatness, with eternal value."

He said he was going to take a walk and would be back in a couple of hours to check on me. He let me know that I had all day, that there was no pressure. He also said that it wasn't my job to identify the dream or fears, that if I would just listen, 33:3 would happen. "It's a promise from God, and you can count on it," he said.

I found a majestic oak next to the oat patch that fit my mission. I spotted a nice patch of grass to sit on and leaned back against the trunk of this purveyor of time. Utopia is in the middle of nowhere, and this spot was about five miles from Utopia. So you could say I was five miles from nowhere.

It was so quiet that I could almost hear the wings of the butterflies that were dancing wistfully between the rain lilies. Dragon flies, the helicopters of the insect world, moved about the oat patch in military fashion. Doves dove into the field, seemingly out of nowhere, seeking seed and gravel while the Vermillion Flycatcher found his fill from flying insects as he appeared to be shagging flies from the cedar posts. Thus I watched and observed creation, soaking it in, marveling at the miracles of life. All this was just a prelude to the Voice.

In this attitude and posture of thanks and marvel, the worries of the world fell aside, allowing me to connect with the Artist, the Maestro of this symphony of life displayed just for me at this moment in the history of time. I could sense there was a direct correlation between disconnecting from the noise of the world and receiving revelation. A soft breeze enveloped me with the fragrant aroma of earth's mixing bowl. In that moment He spoke—the Creator, the Designer of life. I heard it in my heart, in the deep place of my Spirit. It wasn't audible; it was clearer than that. It was peace-provoking and weighty in a good sense, like the weight of a warm quilt on a cold night.

"Golf is not your vocation; it is your platform. It is a place for sowing seeds of light, hope, and life, especially inside the ropes on tournament day where most players check out, allowing the selfishness of the moment and pressure of the day to close the door to true adventure and revelation.

"Don't be afraid of the new swing. It is part of your platform, and it will set you apart. It will inspire seekers of truth in all walks of life to open the locked vault of false tradition's stronghold. You will speak greatness into many as I flood you with insight. You will live life as a noticer as you listen to me. You will bring life where there is death, light where there is darkness, hope where there is pain, and freedom to those trapped in fear.

"Your fear is that if you do this, you will miss out, that you will not play well, that you will be wasting a career, and that you will look like a fool. But I say, when you choose this path you will find life; you will be filled to overflowing with what victory can't deliver. When you forget about yourself and focus on those with whom I cross your path, your performance will soar and you will play fearlessly, knowing neither failure nor victory has any hold on you. You will be relentlessly competitive yet full of grace, tenacious yet full of peace. And if you trust me instead of resisting, like Johnny's horses, you will receive soul freedom."

I knew I had just received a recipe for the true zone, a performance zone that defied typical wisdom. The revelation came in like a 220 current to a 110 outlet.

There is no experience like receiving a revelation, a call to greatness. No victory, no treasure, no person or object can compete with the overwhelming sense of security created by the Voice. The heart beats differently, a breath is more pure, the colors more alive in that moment. To know that the God of the universe is close and personal changes the game. This was indeed the confirmation I had prayed for.

I had received salvation and freedom on Easter morning; today I received my place in the game. Everyone has a place in the game. The insidious lies of the dream-thief have relegated most to an unfulfilled destiny, wasted seed in a lifeless planter.

To know that I was called to bring freedom to the precious contents of the rusty seed bins of life was profound. I had a simple choice: faith or fear. There was no other option. I chose faith, and in that instant a new dream-guardian was born. No longer was I afraid of the U.S. Open. It was but a platform along the journey of significance.

So on that day I planted my dream seed five miles from nowhere. It became an open door to everywhere.

● Johnny's U.S. Open ●

Chapter 10

On day six of my visit to Utopia I showed up at the range, hoping to play golf. But Johnny surprised me yet again. After I had hit balls for an hour, he walked up with a young golfer from Utopia.

"This here is Danny. He wants to be on the golf team at the high school and wants some help on his swing. Says he is willing to do anything to get better. I told him about you—that you have a new swing and the secret to the game to teach him. I'll see you boys later," said Johnny as he winked at me and walked off.

My first thought was that this was an intrusion upon my time. However, the call to greatness at the seed bin had given me new eyes. I caught myself and instead became intrigued with the purpose of this encounter.

"Thank you for spending time with me," Danny said. "My dad left our family a few years back, and Johnny has been like a father to me. Without the Links of Utopia golf course and Johnny, I don't know what would have happened to me. Johnny says you have the secret to the game. I'm ready to learn."

I was humbled by the openness and yearning in Danny's spirit. What I heard under the tree near the oat field was now unfolding. It was a privilege to die to my agenda and adopt His.

"Let's see what you've got," I said with a smile. "Take out your six iron and hit a few to get warmed up."

"Yes, sir," Danny said enthusiastically.

As he was warming up, I could tell he was a beginner. But he showed some athleticism. Unfortunately, his shots were flying everywhere, mostly to the right and short. The ground where he was hitting looked like an armadillo had been digging for grubs. This kid needed some serious help.

"How long you been playing the game?" I asked.

"Less than a year. I just finished eighth grade and Johnny thinks I could play for the team as a freshman next fall if I practice hard this summer. Johnny loaned me these clubs and said if I work hard on my game and help him around the course, I can keep them. Says he needs to see conviction from me first."

That brought a smile to my face. "Yep, he is big on conviction," I said with a chuckle.

Right off the bat I could see how difficult it was for a new student to synchronize everything in the swing. Could it be that the Utopia Pre-Set was a great method for teaching new students? Then it hit me: That was exactly Johnny's point in having me give Danny a lesson. Or was it?

I noticed that between warm-up shots, Danny was staring into a distant field.

"You O.K.?" I asked, to see if there was something on his mind.

"I'm great," he replied as if my question brought him back to the range.

"O.K., on this one, stop your backswing at the top," I instructed.

When he did, his right elbow was flying, his wrist wasn't hinged, the club was laid off, and his body had barely rotated. On top of that, he picked the club up, he leaned forward on the backswing, and his right shoulder lifted. This swing was at best a dreaded slice in the making—if he somehow managed to get back to the ball from there. There was a good chance as well that he would hit it fat with the reverse pivot that was inevitable.

"This good?" he asked.

"Well, Danny, let's make a couple changes here," I replied as I hinged his wrist, got the club head on plane, dropped in his right elbow and shoulder, rotated his body, and had his weight shift back to the inside of his right foot.

"Yeah, that looks a little bit better," I said with a chuckle.

"I'm sorry, what did you say?" he replied while looking off into the next field again.

"That looks good now," I returned, slightly annoyed by his drifting attention. "How does it feel?"

"Uncomfortable," he laughed.

"That's O.K. Sometimes good things are uncomfortable," I stated as I kicked the ball out of the way. "This is a golfer's position. Swing down as if there were a ball there. Just let your arms release and body turn just as if you were swinging a baseball bat."

As he did, he instinctively leaned right, dropping his right shoulder, causing the club to dig deep into the ground.

"O.K., take it to the top again. You're going to like this," I said.

I got him into the position again. I had him shut his eyes.

"Now, picture a baseball pitcher throwing the ball. Swing as if you were hitting a low pitch to left field and hold your finish," I coached.

His left foot actually stepped slightly into the pitch as he made a great move through the ball. You could hear the speed of the club head as it rotated through. His finish was high and left over his shoulder and his belt buckle was pointing to left field.

"O.K., open your eyes," I said just as the horses in the distant field began to run and buck and carry on as if they had caught his make-believe towering fly ball.

"Wow," he replied enthusiastically.

"Yeah, that's the way a golf swing is supposed to feel." I said feeling as if we had just crossed a hurdle.

"Look at that palomino. Wow! They are running free!" he said, completely absorbed in this Old West scene of playful horses.

Danny had just entered the world of his true passion. I realized that he had been watching these horses in the distance from the moment he arrived. He was not responding to my self-proclaimed great coaching; he was responding with his heart to something that captured his imagination.

I had a choice. Get frustrated and demand his attention. Or observe his eyes, listen to his heart, and lead him on a true search for his passion.

"Let's go watch," I said as we dropped the clubs and walked

quickly the 300 or so yards to the fence.

"Look at that one prancing and rearing!" he said with wide eyes and a smile. "That is one powerful, magnificent creature."

I leaned on a fence post and put my foot up on the bottom strand of the wire. "Danny, what is your passion in life?" I asked.

"Golf," he said, while never taking his eyes off the dancing horses.

"Why do you like golf so much?" I followed.

"Well, Johnny says I can be good and make the team and earn some clubs. I love Johnny and want to make him proud," he replied.

I could see what was happening. His dad had left a hole in his heart and Johnny had been inserted. His aching need for approval had been transferred to Johnny because of the pain. Acceptance and approval had blinded him from his true passion.

"Danny, is there anything you love more than golf? I asked.

He looked at me, a little confused as if it were a trick question. "I don't think so?" he replied hesitantly.

"What are we doing out here today?" I pressed.

"Taking a golf lesson," he replied as several of the horses came bolting over towards us. It was as if they were racing to see who could get to Danny first. I watched in awe as they bypassed me and went right to him. He reached out his hand and touched their faces as if to say, Thanks for making my day.

"No, we are watching horses," I said with a chuckle.

"Oh, I'm sorry," he said, a little embarrassed as he turned to head back to the range.

The horses shook their heads and whinnied at him.

"What about them?" I asked without budging off of the fence.

He turned back and stared at the horses from several feet away. They stared at him as if to penetrate the pain and ask the same question: "Danny, what is your passion?"

He slowly stepped toward the horses and then buried his face in theirs, nuzzling his cheeks up against theirs while patting their necks. It was a moment to savor. Two different natures were coming together in an understanding of calling. The horses could sense that he was a horseman; the question was, could he?

After a while he looked at me and said, "He broke a promise. He broke my heart."

I didn't say a word, even though I didn't understand. At that moment I just listened.

"My dad promised me a horse when I was young. He never followed through, and then he just left," he revealed through eyes swollen with tears.

"I love horses," Danny continued. I have always loved horses. I want to ride them, train them, own them. I want the biggest horse ranch in Texas. I want to watch a colt being born and then ride him one day. Horses are my passion," he blurted out to his surprise.

By now most of the herd had trotted to the fence. Danny started stroking their necks and cheeks. The horses loved him; it was a privilege to watch this scene unfold.

After a few minutes the alpha came streaking across the field. As he closed in, he started rearing and bucking and nipping at all the horses, causing them to exit in a mad dash. The alpha then bolted toward Danny, stopping in a spray of dirt just before the fence. He snorted loudly, reared and whinnied, then turned on a dime and sprinted away as if to make it clear, this was his herd.

I watched Danny's reaction. He smiled and said, "He has a passion for his herd. He just wanted me to know that."

"Do you?" I asked as we turned to head back toward the range.

Danny was struck to the heart by this question. It wasn't a question as much as it was an invitation into his calling. It was his defining moment. He stopped and looked back at the horses squinting as the wheels inside his head were turning. After a moment he looked at me with conviction in his eyes and said, "Yes."

He knew that he had just found his dream seed. "Thank you, Mr. Luke," he said with a heart of thanks.

"Let's go tell Johnny," I suggested, knowing that horses trumped golf.

"Oh, no, he'll be disappointed," Danny worried.

"No, he'll be thrilled. He's a dream-guardian," I said with a grin.

"A what?" he questioned.

"You'll see," I said with a wink and a smile.

We walked toward the backside of the barn where Johnny and Grace often sat under the canopy of the big willow taking in the wonder of this place. As we rounded the corner, there they were, sitting, laughing and sharing a father-daughter moment.

Johnny looked over at us, rounding the barn and didn't miss a beat. "What took you so long?" he said with a chuckle.

He knew his stuff. He knew the lesson wasn't just about me teaching a swing, though that was important. He believed that having me teach the method would force me to a deeper level of conviction and understanding of the Pre-Set swing. But he also knew that the secret of which he spoke was about passion. The lesson was a set-up, both for me and Danny.

"So, what's up, boys?" he kidded.

I looked over at Danny and said to Johnny, "This young man just discovered his true passion and needs some help stepping into his destiny."

"Is that true, son?" Johnny asked Danny.

"Yes, sir. I'm sorry I didn't tell you before," he said.

"Didn't tell me what?" Johnny pressed.

"Well, I like golf and all that. I, I, I just love horses more. I want to be a horse trainer. I never thought that was possible, because we don't have money or land."

"Well, my, oh my. You didn't think I knew that? On the holes next to the horse pastures your foot has never once touched the fairway. Your best shots happen there as you focus and hit the ball purposely next to the fence perfectly each time. You then walk next to the fence, staring at the grazing horses." Johnny spoke with a smile and gleam in his eye. "I have just been waiting for you to discover the object of your dream."

"You really noticed?" Danny asked sheepishly.

"Son, you are a horseman. It's written all over you. How about, instead of clubs, we trade your summer of work for a horse," Johnny said with joy. "And you can keep him at our place 'til you get a place of your own one day."

Danny couldn't speak. His mouth hung open in disbelief.

"Grace, you have need for an apprentice this summer?" Johnny asked, looking over at his radiant daughter.

"Yes, sir, and I have a shovel just his size over by that wheelbarrow," she said with a laugh. "Danny, let's start today with mucking the stalls and feeding the horses."

Johnny chimed in, "And tomorrow at 8:00 we'll meet at the round pen for a lesson with the black stallion. I'll share the secret of the round pen with you then."

Turning to me he said, "Luke, I'd like it if you could join us for your final lesson before you leave. I have a little gift for you as well."

"Yes, sir. I look forward to it," I replied.

Grace turned to Danny and said, "Come on, let me show you around." The two of them headed for the lowest yet most important task of each day: the cleaning of the stalls.

Johnny slapped me on the back as he stood. "Tomorrow you'll have your answer."

"To what?" I asked.

"To the question you asked me the other day: How do I do it?" he replied.

"I'll be right back," he said as he headed into the barn. Johnny left me in deep thought for a moment.

Life was beautiful, and I was at peace in Utopia. The sun was warm on my back as the hens pecked around for seed, a bluebird sat like a hood ornament on the cement cistern, and the kittens were sword-fighting with their shadows. I was settled, yet excited. And, to be honest, I was anticipating the final lesson from Johnny.

Johnny walked out of the barn with two fly rods and a tackle box. "Hey, now that you ran your student off, you wanna wet a line?" he asked with a smile.

"Are you kidding? Maybe we can catch Toby off-guard again!" I exclaimed, thinking back to the bass I caught underwater the last time we fished together.

Johnny threw the poles and tackle box into the back of his truck. Then he reached out with both hands, putting them on my shoulders. He looked into my eyes as he said, "Good job this morning. You were a noticer. You let go of your agenda to hear a deeper voice. Son, that is special."

"Thank you. That means a lot coming from you. I'm happy for

Danny. Even though he just traded his six-iron for a poop shovel," I said with a laugh.

Johnny chuckled as he started his truck. "He shouldn't have any synchronization issues with the shovel!"

As we drove off, heading for the Sabinal, he looked out into the pasture and said, "Looks like a great day for fishing. The cows are grazing, and the wind is from the south."

"Really?" I asked. "You can tell by the cows and wind?"

Johnny replied by reciting a verse from his granddad,

"When the wind is from the north, the fisherman shan't go forth. When the wind is from the east, the fish bite the least. When the wind is from the west, the fishin' is best. And when the wind is from the south, the bait floats right into the fish's mouth."

"I like that," I said with a grin. "What about the cows?"

"Oh, that," he laughed. "It's just some old wives' tale, probably. But it makes good copy."

"Well, my granddad taught me a verse as well," I said.

"Go for it," Johnny said with delight.

I recited:

>"Lord, give me grace
>To catch a fish
>So big that even I
>When telling of it afterwards

May never need to lie.

A question I would ask you
And a truthful answer wish
Are all fisherman liars,
And do only liars fish?

Since a question you have asked
And a truthful answer wish
All men are liars,
And some fish."

Johnny let out a belly laugh and reached over and slapped me on the knee. I smiled deeply as great friends do when they are just shooting the breeze. And so we bumped along the caliche road with fishing on our minds, windows down, gravel flying, and Rascal Flats on the radio.

Chapter 11

It was my last morning in Utopia. I had been anticipating the final lesson throughout the night. I packed the car with both sadness and exhilaration: sadness that I had to leave Utopia; exhilaration that I had a line in the sand to cross at the U.S. Open.

After a couple eggs over easy, sausage, hash browns, biscuits and gravy and a cup of coffee at the café, I headed to my rendezvous with the crew down at the round pen. I arrived just as Grace was leading the black stallion into the pen. Danny and I climbed up on the fence to watch the show. Johnny was standing in the middle of the round pen. "Morning, boys," he said as he tipped his hat.

Grace took the halter off the horse and let him roam free as she closed the gate and joined us on the fence. He seemed fairly calm. Instinctively, it seemed, he started jogging around the pen. Johnny remained in the center of the ring, holding the six-foot bamboo rod with a red bandanna fastened on the end. At this point he wasn't pointing the bamboo at the horse, just holding it like a caddy would a flagstick.

Johnny watched the horse and followed the stallion's eyes with his. He slowly turned like the center of a carousel. The horse was aware of his presence. Johnny raised the tip of the pole and pointed it directly at the horse. The stallion's speed increased. Johnny then pointed the pole in front of the horse, which caused the horse to turn and sprint in the other direction. Johnny cut him off a few more times, but on this morning the stallion was not foaming and angry. It looked as though he was just obeying. Now for the test.

Johnny lowered both the bandanna and his shoulder and turned his head and body away from the horse. The stallion stopped and watched. Johnny took a step away from the center in the opposite direction from the horse and began to walk. To our amazement, the horse followed. He worked his way to within three feet of Johnny and stayed at that distance as they walked around the pen. Johnny then stopped and turned looking into the eyes of the stallion. They stood nose to nose. Johnny reached up and stroked the neck of the horse.

Johnny then unfastened the red bandanna from the end of the bamboo rod. The stallion watched with great interest. After all, that bandanna had been the object of its fear until now. He then began to gently rub the bandanna across the horses' face, eyes, ears, and neck.

While the stallion seemed agitated at first, it nevertheless put up with the intrusion into its space. Johnny then rubbed it across its back and legs and chest. He returned to the face and waved the bandanna in front of his eyes, allowing it to brush the horse's face and eyes. Next, he waved it wildly all around the head and face, while the great stallion stood motionless.

Then Johnny knelt and carefully tied the bandanna around its front leg, the one with the white foot. The stallion dropped its head to see its new accessory wrapped around its cannon bone. It stamped its hoof with curiosity more than agitation then began to follow Johnny around the pen. It was evident that Johnny had led this stallion to freedom.

Grace jumped down from the fence and put the halter back on the compliant horse and led him to his stall. Johnny asked us to meet him at the picnic table. We could hear Grace quietly singing to the stallion in the background.

Danny and I were quiet as we moved to the other side of the barn where the shade of the trimmed willow branches provided an umbrella for the inviting wooden picnic table. Johnny joined us and began his final lesson.

"This stallion was never ridden by a cowboy," Johnny reiterated from the other day. "He was at his athletic best with a spurred cowboy on his back and a flank-strap around his belly. Bucked them all. He was a legend. He was notorious throughout Texas."

"What do you think about the rodeo?" Danny asked curiously.

"I love the rodeo. Contrary to what folks might think, bronc horses are treated with great love and respect. Their owners coddle them, feed them well, and provide a great life for them. These horses have been bred to jump and buck. They are respected and applauded for their great athleticism. Their inbred job is to remove a cowboy from their back. The good ones do just that, to the chagrin of the cowboy. Horses just have instincts that they react to," he said. "All horses have to be freed from their defense system of fleeing before they can be ridden. These bronc horses just have never been trained for riding. So they do what they know how to do, buck and flee. In the end, it isn't the horse that limps out of the stadium, it's the cowboy."

We all laughed at that visual.

"When their rodeo days are over, we free them for their new purpose in life: to bring joy to people, especially children," Johnny continued. "When horses and people are born, they have a tendency to fear each other at first. It is a beautiful thing when they learn to love and respect each other."

Danny added, "I have a family video of me crying when I was two because I was afraid of horses. My mom was proudly holding me in her lap in the saddle on my first ride."

115

"Who would have known that horses would become your passion in life?" I added.

We all chuckled in amazement.

"Freedom begins in the round pen," Johnny instructed. "It isn't that dangerous to be in the pen with an unridden horse. Their first instinct is to run, not bite or kick. But you always take a pole or whip in with you so the animal respects you and so you have a line of defense in case it is the one in a hundred that is overly aggressive."

He tacked on, "And it helps to be able to climb a fence quickly!"

"Let's head back over to the pen," he said as he grabbed the bamboo rod and fastened a new red bandanna to the end.

I unlatched the gate and we all entered as he continued to teach.

"You have to enter the pen completely mentally prepared," Johnny cautioned. "An attitude of confidence must exude from your expressions, while grace and compassion lead your emotions. Anger or fear will prolong the battle and send the wrong messages. Horses really do have horse sense; they know what you are feeling inside."

"This round pen is where the horse is forced to face his fears and deal with chaos. During the training period, the red bandanna becomes the focal point to freedom for the horse. Initially a wild horse would rather spend his days running from predators and foraging for survival lost in the pecking order of a random herd than submit to the trainer. However, when the horse submits to and receives the bandanna, freedom replaces chaos, trust replaces the prey's fear, and purpose replaces aimless running."

"Here is the secret to the round pen: Greatness can only happen when we face and dismantle our fears. The red bandanna starts out as an object of fear but ends up as a symbol of freedom."

Johnny then turned his attention to Danny, entering him into the story, "Danny, your daddy most likely fled the family because of fear. Fear from the dream-taker's constant condemnation that he wasn't good enough, not a good provider, that he was a poor husband and father, that he was a loser in life. Fleeing the bandanna is where he has settled."

As Danny stared off into the distant fields, Johnny reached out his hand and placed it on his shoulder. He waited. When Danny looked back to him, Johnny spoke with passion. "But fleeing stops with you. You aren't here by accident, and this summer is your personal round pen. In the end, like all of us, you'll have to decide if you want to embrace the bandanna. And who knows? Your choice just might bring freedom to your dad one day."

It was a beautiful moment for Danny. Johnny continued, "You'll see a lot of the round pen this summer. We'll head to the rescue center Monday to pick up your new horse. He'll need a lot of love and patience."

"Are you serious?" Danny asked trying to control his enthusiasm.

"Yep! Johnny exclaimed with his cowboy smile. "In the meantime I suspect Grace has some work for you, and we need to get Luke on the road."

Danny thanked Johnny and Grace for caring enough to give him the chance. He then looked over at me and said with a big grin on his face, "Thanks for the golf lesson." Everyone laughed, knowing he hadn't heard a word I said about golf.

Johnny led us out of the pen and back over to the tack room where he got another bandanna. He tossed it to me saying, "This is for you. When I taught you the Pre-Set, I said that it was the first secret to freedom in the chaos. This is the second. Keep it where you can see it. When fear comes knocking, choose freedom instead. See His face, Feel His presence, trust His love."

"Thanks, Johnny; I have a good spot for it," I said as I twirled it tightly and wrapped it around my left wrist a couple of times and tied it off. "It seemed to work for the stallion," I said as everyone laughed.

We headed to my truck. Danny shook my hand and thanked me again.

Grace gave me a hug and said, "It's been a pleasure."

I responded, "The pleasure was all mine. Thanks for sharing the story of TK with me. I'll be watching for an open door with him."

"Don't be surprised," she replied with an expectant smile.

I turned to Johnny and said, "What a week."

"This is the way life is supposed to be lived," he replied. "Go claim your bean field."

"OK, we can have some lentil soup upon my return," I joked.

They all laughed and off I drove, heading for the majesty of the U.S. Open with a goat ranch golf course in my rear view mirror. Life is funny that way, when you receive rather than resist the red bandanna. Nothing is as it seems. I was glad to have new eyes that took me beyond reality to the place of parables, a place where the supernatural settles upon the natural, revealing the true story being written.

118

Chapter 12:

In a bizarre freak of nature back in March, this year's U.S. Open venue was destroyed by a disastrous flood and subsequent fire to the clubhouse. In an unprecedented move, the tournament committee had to re-direct the U.S. Open to a new venue. Because it happened at the last minute, they had to break their tradition of using only the old, venerable sites of past Opens.

In a stroke of genius, the tournament committee created a contingency plan that delighted the players and ignited great anticipation among the fans for this year's last-minute venue. They chose the Patriot Club in Tulsa, Oklahoma, an extraordinary course dedicated to the honor of our armed forces. The distinguished Folds of Honor organization is housed at the club and uses golf to raise millions of dollars to help educate the children and spouses of our fallen and wounded soldiers. Each day at 1:00 p.m., 1300 in military time, play is halted for 13 chimes from the bell tower. These chimes symbolize the 13 folds of the flag given to the family of those who gave their lives for freedom. The tournament officials agreed to embrace this tribute during the tournament each day. They also dedicated two spots in the Patriot Club U.S. Open to current or former members of our armed forces. The stage was set for this Open to capture the attention of the world with its unique focus and venue.

While I had played in five events on the PGA Tour, they paled in comparison to the size and scope of the U.S. Open. Outside the ropes, this place looked like a disrupted fire ant bed. Thank goodness my place was inside the ropes.

There is a peacefulness that all athletes experience when they walk into their world, their court. It is the place where their gifts are on display, where they feel most comfortable in life. As David Robinson, the great former San Antonio Spur and NBA Hall of Famer once said, "Walking on the court is like stepping onto my childhood playground."

Initially, the media was oblivious to me, a relative no-name in this event. That allowed me the privilege of learning the course and preparing in obscurity. Who could have imagined a course in Tulsa with such hills and canyons? The first tee was a near-replica of the Obra Maestra cliff, with vistas for miles and a fall of several hundred feet to the fairway in a perfectly sculpted canyon below. The course was a unique combination of mountain, woodland, and bottom-land links golf, all brought together through the imagination of the course design team and nature's great artist.

The Patriot Club included 7400 yards of tight zoysia fairways lined by four- to eight-inch fescue rough. Several spring-fed creeks meandered relentlessly through the property, forcing risk-reward decisions at every turn. The elevated bent greens were running 13 during the practice rounds, with sideboards shaved down like a Chihuahua. The wind swirled unpredictably through the canyons, blew incessantly on the tops of the hills, and remained relatively calm below the tree line in the heavy woodlands. Club selection became a meteorological science. The heat index would be nearly 105 degrees. This was going to be a test that measured up to the standards of the warriors to whom this facility was dedicated.

Johnny encouraged me to come to the Patriot Club a week early, which allowed me to learn this first-time venue as well as any competitor. That was a major advantage for me and other rookies this year. I continued the practice of hiring an experienced local caddy at each tournament site. This ingratiated me to the locals and served to create a small but growing fan base. It also helped me learn the course quickly, and it set me apart from the other players as I embraced a bygone positive tradition from the history of the game.

When I first got to the range, I was one of about ten players at the course. I was eager to unveil my new swing and work through the self-consciousness before the tournament began. The local pro provided me with a caddy who was a fighter pilot now serving in the air national guard. He spent his days caddying at the Patriot Club and playing in high-level amateur tournaments when he wasn't deployed or training as a defender of freedom. His call name was Sky, and that is how he introduced himself. I smiled big as I chuckled at God's supernatural ways. I told him about the horse that had taken me to Obra Maestra.

Sky smiled and said that he was a believer, a code name between those who see the supernatural descending upon the natural. And so the hand of God brought two faith sojourners together for an encounter with a line in the sand.

He shared the story of how he got his name. During fighter-pilot school one of the assignments was to write an in-depth paper about the source of his passion. For years this was a feared project, as the commanding officer would rip to shreds the superficial contents of most of the greenhorn jet jockey's papers, pressing them to go deeper until they landed on the true source of their passion. While the other students spent hours poring over their papers, Sky simply wrote one word, "sky." The commanding officer called him to the front of the class at attention. He then began to vehemently challenge him for the audacity of turning in a one-word paper when the other students spent hours on theirs. The officer then asked if he wanted another chance to conform his paper and effort to match the other wannabe pilots.

Sky answered with confidence, "No, sir. The sky is my passion.

121

It's why I fly. I always look up, and I always reach for the stars. And when it's all over, heaven is my final destination."

The commanding officer looked at the others in the class and said, "This is the greatest paper I have ever read. And this, gentlemen, is a man of conviction, courage, and focus. Take note." He then looked at Sky and said, "Sky, take a seat."

Thus his call name was sealed. That moment set him apart from the other cadets and sealed his destiny as one of the greatest fighter pilots of his generation.

I needed unwavering support from my caddy for the mission in front of me. So, before I hit a shot, I surprised Sky by asking him to hit a few balls. He obliged using the traditional swing of the masses. After ten shots, I asked him to hit a few with the Utopia Pre-Set method. I started by telling him it was a drill. He immediately began to hit the ball flush and on a string. I then asked him to go back to his other swing. His shots were good but not as accurate as with the Pre-Set method. Not even close. I asked him to hit a few more with the Pre-Set. He did with straighter and more solid shots.

I took the club from my new convert and began to stripe the ball at my target using the Pre-Set method. I told him that this was not a teaching drill but the way I would be swinging the club at the U.S. Open. He looked amazed then broke out in a wide smile. I invited him to join me on this adventure into the future of golf. He excitedly said the right thing, "I'm your wingman!"

By the time the tournament began, I was an anomaly to the spectators. We were making believers out of many of those who stuck around long enough to watch the swing. The Face-On putting style was also building momentum and interest. With the new ban on the anchoring of the putter, the Face-On putting style provided a legal non-anchoring method for all golfers looking for an option to traditional putting.

Several players stopped by my spot on the range to inquire about the Utopia Pre-Set swing and to try it out. Several others just snickered and joked with other players behind my back. One sour has-been walked up to me and said, "We don't need any more prima donnas out here."

Sky had my back and quickly replied to the veteran with a compliment, "Man, that was the greatest recovery shot on number 17 when you won in Florida eight years ago. What club did you hit?" The shallow veteran, caught off-guard by the compliment and filled with the need for approval, went into great detail about the shot. As he finished, he introduced himself to both of us and said, "Good luck."

As he left, Sky winked at me and said, "A kind word turns away wrath. It opens the door for making a new friend rather than an enemy. And that guy could use a friend; his identity is dying with his game." Sky was a true wingman.

During our practice rounds, Sky had me hit a second ball each day to a spot about 5 to 10 yards short of the green. I asked him why and he said that he suspected an absolute brutal course set-up. He said that it would necessitate hitting the ball short of the green in many cases because of the firmness of the greens. He added that not many players understood that the only flat and somewhat soft areas around the greens were mainly just short.

His final coaching point was that if we were in the thick rough and couldn't quite reach the green, we would know how to play chips and pitches from just short of the green. This was brilliance, as I was to experience once the tournament started. On the practice range I hit hundreds of pitches from 5 to 10 yards off the practice green while others went about their normal routines. My confidence was building.

On the morning of the first day of the tournament I was quietly going through my new game-day routine, hitting a few balls while consciously working on the four-count rhythm. Johnny had coached me to focus on rhythm during my game-day warm-up routine. He said with the extra adrenalin and tension, energy management was the key to hitting great shots on game day.

As Sky tossed me another ball, I noticed TK walking up. He greeted me, then asked about the Pre-Set swing. I thought about what to say for a moment then just cut to the chase, "Johnny says hi, as does Grace."

He turned ashen white as he stood there too stunned to move. He then quietly asked me, "Did he tell you everything?"

"Yes," I replied. "Johnny and Grace cared about you deeply and still do. They were crushed when they never got to see you again. Mostly they were crushed for you and what you went through to become a champion."

"Where are they?" he inquired.

"In Utopia, Texas, living their dream. Johnny owns a ranch and operates a little nine-holer. Teaches cowboys and locals to play the game. He and Grace transform retired bronc horses, wild mustangs, and rescued horses to trail horses and give them to kids to ride," I said.

That brought a smile to TK's face.

"Grace was always a dreamer. She told me one day she was going to train horses and sing," TK said.

"She is doing both because she has a dream-guardian as a father. Just so you know, what your dad meant for harm, God turned into good for Johnny and Grace. Johnny is living his dream as well," I said to help relieve his mind.

"The world thinks I'm living my dream, too." He stopped and looked away as he cleared his throat. "But I'm in prison. Johnny was my teacher and friend. He was more of a father to me than my dad. And I still believe the Pre-Set is superior to any golf swing. You will do well with it here. It's a U.S. Open swing."

"Have you ever thought about going back to it?" I asked.

"My dad has forbidden me to. I'm not sure I could handle the scrutiny and change at this stage of the game. I have sponsors, agents, fans ..." he trailed off.

"Fear," I bravely challenged, "is your true opponent, the mortar of your prison walls. There is a key to freedom. You can have it; I know where it is. You can cross the line with me this week."

Just then TK's agent walked up and said, "Your interview is waiting. Let's go."

TK reached out his hand to shake mine, and as he did he said, "I want to know."

I quickly wrote down Johnny's number and slipped it to him.

"Give him a call. He would love to hear from you," I said.

He thanked me as he tucked it away in his pocket.

As he turned to walk away, I overheard his agent say, "What were you doing with that nut case?"

I watched as TK and his handlers made their way through the maze of fans and media to yet another interview, where the people were starving for the words of a dead man.

Chapter 13

Day one of the U.S. Open shocked the world. The course reminded me of freshman chemistry where the grandiose plans of many a student came crashing down, relegating them to second choice majors.

Never had the scoring average been so high and flame-outs so prevalent. The water had been cut back the day before, leaving the fairways and greens rock hard. The narrow fairways were cut so tight that players had to read the break from the tee box and play clubs to the flat spots. Only those who had taken the time to notice and chart these areas during the practice rounds were surviving.

Sky knew where each trouble spot was and had me hit hybrids to places that left me longer shots into the green, but from the fairway. I trusted him and continued to play patient survival golf. Seldom did I hit a ball past the center of the green. Most of the day I left the ball just short of the greens, as we had practiced, because of the greens' severity. It was imperative to leave the ball below the hole, even if it meant missing the green.

The greens were running 14 on the stimpmeter and were rock hard, nothing like the practice rounds. Few balls hit with a club higher than an eight-iron could hold a green. These were guerilla warfare conditions, where missing the green on purpose was part of the strategy. Most players refused to buy in and were greeted with disaster. They blew up quickly, cursing the course and set-up, rather than playing the game that was given to them.

To survive and win here would require a complete rewiring of the instrument panels, returning to the origins of golf in the pastures of Scotland: get the ball in the hole in fewer strokes than the others. For those who focused on par, a nightmare engulfed them, leaving their fragile identities strewn throughout the Oklahoma landscape known as tornado alley.

Half of the field shot above 80 on day one. Fifteen players refused to post their scores, for fear it would affect their scoring average, choosing instead to withdraw and high-tail it out of the twilight zone back to their comfort zone. Many would never be the same.

In essence, this Open that honored our armed forces, revealed the character necessary to serve in the military. This tournament served as an unfolding boot camp that revealed what each PGA Tour player was made of. True champions were emerging; the mentally tough were surviving. Three over par 75 was leading, and I was one back.

Throughout the day, Sky adjusted expectations according to the conditions and spoke to me about playing the game given to us. He coached on each hole how to get to the flat spots, the places from which to chip uphill, the green bunkers that we actually wanted to be in for our only chance for par. He also did something uncanny. As we walked the fairways, he pointed out several flat places in the rough to aim for in case of emergencies in the coming days. Places of relatively short grass beyond the thick rough, hidden from the undiscerning eye of the conventional player.

On day two, all the players assumed that the course set-up would be easier, greens and fairways syringed to slow them down, tee boxes moved up, and pin places eased. But to everyone's surprise the tournament committee did not lighten up but instead put the hammer down. They were determined to have this tournament find a new breed of champion, a true warrior and survivor. The average score was 82, and the cut line was 164, 20 over par. Never in the history of golf has the scoring been this brutal. Amazingly, the TV ratings were off the charts. I shot another 76 to remain a couple behind.

If it seemed that things couldn't get worse, day three ushered in the winds off of the plains. Temperatures hovered near 105 degrees, and the winds gusted to 30 miles per hour. A steady line of EMS vehicles carried off spectators succumbing to heat-related issues.

Sky kept me hydrated and kept an ice-cold towel around my neck all day long. He was a workhorse and a relentless encourager and strategist. The leaders were caving, making mistakes of impatience because of the conditions and fatigue of the three-day battle. Suddenly I was in the lead. TK, several groups ahead, was making a move as well. By the back nine, TK and I had broken from the field. Pars were like gold, and bogies, silver. The game had been redefined this week as birdies were almost nonexistent.

I made par on every hole coming in, seven of them from playing about five yards short of the green and getting up and down for par. I was one over for the day, four shots in front of TK, and eight in front of the next closest player.

Despite shooting a one over 73, it was definitely the greatest round of golf I had ever played. I had been anonymous until that moment. Now at nine over par, I was leading the U.S. Open.

The media was in a frenzy as I walked in for the post-round interview just as TK, their champion, was about to walk out the back door. When he saw me, something made him pause. He stood unnoticed in the back corner and listened.

The first question posed to me was from a sarcastic reporter looking to discredit my position, "Are you embarrassed about being nine over par and leading by four shots?"

"No," I responded, "I am proud to be leading the U.S. Open, score to par is irrelevant."

"What do you mean?" the reporter pressed, "This week has embarrassed the game of golf and many of the best players in the game."

"Sir," I replied, "this has been a great week for golf. The tournament committee should be commended. It has given us a stern test of character and talent, and that is a good thing for any person in any walk of life. It serves as a reminder to us of what our defenders of freedom go through to become soldiers and win battles. And that is a good thing at this tournament site dedicated to them."

A burst of applause erupted, which shut down this pessimist. A second question was shouted from the back, "What are you trying to prove with your swing? Seems like you are mocking the way the game is supposed to be played."

"I love this game and was taught a better way. Maybe in the end it will help more people enjoy success on the links. That is my desire. By the way, what is the name of the person who told you how the game was supposed to be played?"

Applause again cascaded through the crowd accompanied by a spattering of laughter. But the reporter pressed for more. "You say you were taught. By whom?"

Wanting to protect Johnny's privacy, I used one of his tactics. "Oh, a cowboy down in Texas named Johnny. You can read about him in 1st Samuel 18."

Laughter and amusement followed as a new question and new

angle came. "Tomorrow you will be paired with TK. This is the only major he hasn't won. He shot under par today, the only person in the tournament to do so. What do you think your chances are against TK?"

I glanced in the direction of TK with a smile then quickly returned my focus to the reporter. "Well, first of all, TK is the greatest player of my generation, maybe of all times. I respect him a lot for his play. The good news is," I paused briefly, "I am playing the course, not TK."

Another question about my swing came, "About your unconventional swing. You have hit less than 40 percent of the greens this week. Seems like your swing isn't holding up."

"Well, it's all about perspective," I said. "Maybe I am hitting my targets."

"What do you mean?" he followed.

"I'm playing for score, not greens in regulation," I expressed.

A fashion question I had been anticipating shot from the front of the room, "What's the deal with the red bandanna on your wrist?"

"It's a long story," I stated as I thought of what to say for a moment. "But I think I can do it justice by saying this: A good friend gave it to me as a symbol. The intense pressure, expectations, and fears of competition can steal perspective, causing us to focus on the wrong things. When I look down and see the bandanna out of the corner of my eye at address, my perspective returns and it settles my soul. And when I have the right perspective, I have freedom in the chaos. For me, soul freedom is the key to finding the sweet spot in golf—and in life."

You could tell that I'd hit a chord as the crowd of reporters went silent. Finally, the facilitator spoke into the mic: "One last question."

"What will your secret be to winning tomorrow?" a woman near the podium asked with sincerity.

"Well, it wouldn't be a secret if I told you," I said with a chuckle for comic relief.

As I stood to leave the interview, I reached in my pocket and pulled out my ball and held it up, displaying the letters SFT. "But let's just say it has something to do with SFT," I said as I tossed it to her.

The room thanked me and applauded in appreciation for an interview with spice and depth. Their curiosity was heightened, and they couldn't wait for tomorrow.

As I acknowledged the reporters graciously, my eyes met TK's. And with a touch to the brim of his cap and a nod of thanks, TK exited out the back door.

Chapter 14

The following morning as I arrived at the course, there was general angst in the air about the impending weather. A front was approaching that was predicted to produce massive and severe thunderstorms early in the evening and to last over the next few days. This was typical in Northeastern Oklahoma, known as tornado alley, in the early summer. The officials were hoping to get the round in and praying that there wouldn't be an 18-hole Monday playoff, because of the ominous weather report.

On top of this, TK was nowhere to be found. This was unusual for a player who was obsessed with the same lengthy pre-game routine tournament after tournament. Officials were worried and a search went out, with no one being able to locate him. At 12 minutes before tee-off, his courtesy car appeared at the club. He emerged with an uncharacteristic smile and quickly made his way to the putting green. As he headed for the first tee, he winked at me with a grin as big as Dallas. I had never seen him smile on a golf course, especially in the final round of the U.S. Open.

I followed TK to the first tee, where the official asked us to identify our balls. TK quickly said he was using a Titleist 3 with the letters OM marked in several spots on his ball. He looked at me and said, "I'm coming home. I'm crossing the line with you. I've been in the prison of others' expectations for too long. Let's go have some fun and give 'em a show for the ages. Today I'm painting an Obra Maestra!"

At that moment I understood. He had called Johnny and was re-introduced to the great Artist of life, thus the OM mark. This was indeed going to be one for the ages.

The official pulled me out of my shock, asking me to identify my ball. I said, "Titleist 1 with an SFT mark." The official's eyebrows rose as he wrote it down on his pad.

The next sight floored me. TK was warming up using the Utopia Pre-Set, and he had a Face-On putter in his bag. A murmur spread through the crowd of discerning spectators. As the announcer introduced my name, I realized what was going on. TK had gone to another golf course nearby to warm up with his new, old swing, not wanting anyone to see him, especially his dad, who was in the crowd.

I tried to get my focus but was stunned, to say the least. I teed my ball and took my practice swing from behind the ball as the announcer introduced me.

There was raucous applause from the hundreds of soldiers. They had come out in droves to follow the guy who had acknowledged them in the press and whose comrade was on his bag. On top of that, I had suggested and committed to allow one soldier per hole to walk inside the ropes with me during the final round. They chose men and women who had been wounded in battle for that honor. The tournament officials obliged.

It was a beautiful day of getting to know these heroes and letting them in on what it's like inside the ropes at a major. I let them listen to all of the conversation between Sky and me. It was an honor and privilege to share this experience with those who had sacrificed so much. Johnny and my conversation with the God of Jeremiah 33:3 in the oat patch had taught me well that by sharing life and light inside the ropes, I would be less likely to spiral into the typical self-absorbed tournament pressure. As I listened to these men and women, my pressure paled in comparison to their experiences.

As I approached my ball, the bells of freedom began to chime, catching me by surprise. It was 1:00 p.m. Everything and everyone on the course stopped as we all paid respect to those who had given their lives for the cause of freedom. I felt chills down my spine as the sound of each of the 13 chimes pealed through the great canyons of this venue.

As the final bell chimed, out of nowhere a four-ship of F-16 fighter jets crashed the party, skimming the treetops in a fingertip formation. As they reached the bell tower, the second element leader lit the afterburner, breaking formation. He defied the laws of Sir Isaac Newton, heading straight vertical toward the heavens. It shook the ground and our souls. Watching this incredibly raw patriotic scene, I noticed the warmth on my face as the heat from his afterburner literally fell from the sky. The remaining three jets continued in the missing-man formation as a final tribute to our heroes, eventually disappearing into the Oklahoma horizon. Freedom isn't free.

It took a few moments for the crowd to calm down and for me to compose myself, returning my thoughts to the tournament. I took a deep breath and began again. I initiated the process by painting a masterpiece from behind the ball. As I approached my ball, I took a gunfighter's look at my target then initiated the Pre-Set swing: hinge, plane, turn, turn. I striped the ball down the fairway, thankful for its simplicity and built in four-count metronome in this electrified setting. I hit my target, which was strategically short of the normal landing area.

Instead of pulling his driver, TK chose a three metal. His Pre-Set practice swing caused gasps throughout the crowd. To the delight and surprise of the crowd his ball flew true and just in front of mine. He

135

was determined to copy me and to draft off my decisions. Because I was shorter off the tee in general, I would be hitting first today from the fairway, giving away any secrets, especially when laying up short of the greens. TK and his caddy would be watching every move, often copying my layups, strategically hitting just past me so he could watch how my chips and pitches reacted to the green in terms of break and speed. To his credit, this would give him a huge advantage. He had listened well at the press conference. I smiled on the inside, knowing he was wily like a fox.

On the way to our drives, TK confided to me that he had indeed called Johnny the evening before and was about to embark on a spiritual journey with Johnny. TK said he was committed to listen and to regain the derailed destiny of his life. He went on to say that he had underestimated the power of biblical faith in all aspects of life, including performance.

He then grabbed my forearm, stopping me for a moment in the middle of the fairway. He took off his cap in a gesture of respect and said, "You, my friend, are a hero to me. You stepped across the line first, giving me the courage to follow. I'll always be indebted to you for showing me the way to freedom." Then he put his hat on and put his arm around my shoulder as we started to walk. He whispered in my ear with a chuckle, "But for now, I've got to kick your tail and win the Open!" We both laughed.

Then I shot back, "Like you did at the Texas Open!"

With a smile and grimace, TK mimicked an arrow going into his heart and acted like he was going to fall to the ground. He said, "Ouch. I guess I deserved that."

It was remarkable to see this man freed from prison. No one had ever seen him smile and kid around while playing the game, much less the U.S. Open. He bravely did it with the swing of his youth that took the world by surprise. However, it was the swing of truth that had been stuck in the seed bin of his heart since his record-breaking victory in Houston when he was 13 years old.

TK drafted off me early and caught me on the front nine. He made up two shots on one hole where I misread the chip in both direction and speed. TK watched carefully. He hit his shot from just in front of my ball and proceeded to chip in for birdie. I shot two over for the nine, he shot two under. To the delight of the crowds and television networks, there was a tie at the U.S. Open. We were having fun despite the hardest set-up in U.S. Open history.

We had left the pack in the dust. We were now eight shots in front of the field. It was like the famous battle between Nicklaus and Watson at Turnberry in '77. There was a spiritual bond between us, forged by a man named Johnny, who was wrong about one thing: His masterpiece was still alive and well with TK. I wished he could be here to see this.

We matched shot for shot on the back nine until number 16. Sky was brilliant with the reads and strategies along the way. The Utopia Pre-Set proved to hold together under the brutal conditions. We came to 16 tied. Sky had something up his sleeve for our relentlessly drafting competitor. The pin placement today was such that, barring a miracle, no shot would hold the green. If it did, it would be in a spot for a guaranteed three-putt. And to make things worse, our conservative layup just in front of the green on our approach shot would be problematic.

We drove the ball to our normal layup position in the fairway with TK driving his just in front of us. Sky held me back on the tee box, allowing TK and his caddy to get well down the fairway before Sky delivered his plan. Earlier in the week he had shown me a spot deep in the left rough about pin high over the heads and beyond where the crowd was standing that would provide the only angle that would hold the green. It was the only angle that allowed a player to hit into the slope of the green, the only way to hold this green on a day like this. It would be a gamble because I would have to hit the spot without it looking obvious. We practiced the shot earlier in the week without the crowds. I would have to trust Sky and my skill to pull this off.

We approached the ball, and Sky gave me the number. While the hole wasn't that long, it was beyond treacherous, especially today. I had 175 to what amounted to a green-sized area of soft but thin grass about 20 yards to the left of the green and pin high.

I made the motion of a fade with my hand to Sky in such a way everyone, including TK, knew my intention. However, as I aimed slightly left for the anticipated fade, I played for a slight high draw. The ball came off perfectly.

To the surprise of everyone including TK, the ball disappeared over the top of the crowd to a loud groan in the gallery. There was a quick sprint from the spectators to surround the ball. TK had an issue. He could see the pin placement and knew it was impossible. He was used to following me to the layup area just short, but hadn't been there before. He and his caddie conferred. He assumed that I had made a mistake and mishit the shot. They decided to lay up to the flat spot just in front of the green

We found our ball sitting nicely in an area of worn but soft grass. I had a direct shot at the pin. The huge mound in the green would serve as a back stop behind it to funnel my ball back should it not check, which was doubtful from this close to the green with a fluffy lie. I played a lob to about 10 feet short of the hole. The ball took a con-crete-like bounce to the hole before it grabbed. It proceeded about ten feet past the hole and up the backstop, to the groan of the crowd. But then it began to roll back down the hill right at the hole. The crowd sensed the impending possibilities and began to yell and scream at the ball to go in. It stopped six inches above the hole to the loudest roar of the day for a tap-in par on a hole that averaged a half stroke over par for the day.

TK walked up to the green to see what he had left. His ball would be accelerating over and down the hill if he hit any type of bump-and-run with nothing to stop its momentum. It would be doubtful he could hold the green with any shot. He chose a gutsy flop shot, aiming below the hole where he had a chance at having the ball stop 15 to 20 feet below the hole. He had a very tight lie. This was going to be something if he pulled it off. I had seen him hit a similar shot on the 18th at the Texas Open.

The crowd was hushed as he approached his ball. With the touch of velvet and the swing speed of a driver, TK played a masterful shot that landed a foot beyond the hole, to the delight of the crowd. The ball checked then began its inevitable trickle down the imperceptible slope, stopping at about 15 feet below the hole. His putt narrowly came up short, giving me a one-stroke lead with two to go.

Walking to the next hole, TK said, "Good thing you didn't hit your layup spot on that hole."

I replied with a grin and a wink, "Maybe I did."

We tied 17, a par three, leaving us one hole to play. I still had a one-shot lead. The crowd was huge, engulfing the hole. The mood was electric, as TK and I had given the spectators a memorable show. But it wasn't over. Not by a long shot.

● Johnny's U.S. Open ●

Chapter 15

The dark, anvil-shaped clouds were building quickly on the distant horizon, and the discerning ear could hear thunder. It looked like we would finish the round, but the spectators would have to hustle to get off the property before the storm hit. The officials were doing everything they could to keep the pace of play moving, a monumental feat with the difficulty of the set-up.

The long par-four finishing hole, affectionately named the Black Hole, was treacherous. There was a huge, deep canyon in front and left that spanned the length of the hole with the green set just on the left edge some 525 yards away. They had created a new tee box just for the Open that made our knees shake. The player was forced to traverse the canyon twice. On the drive, the canyon angles away to the right, allowing you to bite off as much as you want to chew.

But disaster awaited, with the smallest tug to the left as the fairway fell off toward the red stakes of the hazardous black hole. To the right was a thick forest. For those that found the fairway, the approach shot back over the canyon was from 225 yards or so, with the ball above your feet.

Today the pin was cut back right. The concrete-like green was only about 10 steps deep where the pin was positioned, with the canyon in the front and a bunker beyond. The margin of error for a shot from over 200 yards was almost non-existent. It would take the skill of a fighter pilot landing on an aircraft carrier at night in the raging North Atlantic Ocean.

On this final hole a double-amputee soldier sat in a wheelchair, awaiting his time inside the ropes with me. He was a former high school state champion in golf. He reached up with his massive arms and gave me a hug, thanking me for allowing him to watch up close and personal. He had a red bandanna tied around both of his wrists. I was moved deeply by this man. At the prick of the Spirit in my soul, I told him that he was my caddy on this hole and that Sky had been relegated to spectator. Sky happily put the clubs across the arms of the wheelchair and backed off, to the disbelief of the soldier. Sky was thrilled. He knew how much this would mean to the soldier.

TK and I both split the fairway off the tee. Because the clubs got in the way of our hero from turning his wheels by himself, he needed a little help. TK pushed on one side, and I, the other. Off we went on a glorious moment of grace in front of thousands upon thousands of fans, applauding not for us, but for this hero that was tagging along inside the ropes on the final hole of one of the greatest U.S. Opens in history.

As usual, I had to hit my second shot first. I had 225 to the pin, 215 to the middle of the green. The tournament had come down to this hole. If I hit for the middle of the green and played for par, it would force TK to fire for the flag in hopes of a miracle birdie to tie me. He had 205 to the flag from a hanging lie.

I discussed the strategy with my new caddie. We decided to hit to the middle, leaving us a 30 to 40-foot treacherous putt. Even though it was to the middle, anything short of the green was in the canyon and anything long left an impossible up and down from the bunker or deep rough.

I pulled my club, a hybrid 4-iron. I took a deep breath and painted a masterpiece from behind the ball. As I walked into the shot I said, "See it," while bearing down on the target like a gunfighter. As my eyes returned to the ball I began the Pre-Set swing. My lips moved as I expressed the words and embraced one of the gifts that Johnny had promised that day on the range in Utopia two weeks ago, the four-count rhythm.

First, I said, "hinge," as I raised the toe of the club, setting my left wrist perfectly in a power position. I then said, "plane," as I slightly rotated the toe of the club to 45 degrees. Next, I relaxed and said, "turn," as I turned around my spine to the top, then repeated the word turn one more time as I initiated the downswing in the context of a perfect four-count rhythm. The sensation of the sweet spot is just that: sweet. It is easy to feel, hard to describe. That sweet sensation was coursing through my system as I watched the beautiful arc of a well-struck hybrid on its path to the center of the penal green. I was indeed grateful for the two gifts Johnny had promised on the range in Utopia: accuracy and rhythm. Most of all I was thankful for freedom in the chaos.

My caddy reached out for a fist bump while attempting to restrain his emotions. I obliged.

It was now TK's turn. Being one down and needing a birdie to tie, he smiled as he pulled his club. He looked over at me and my caddy and said, "That makes this an easy decision." He was taking dead aim at the hole. But this time, unlike the Texas Open, I could tell he was having fun.

From 205 to the back pin, he chose to take an extra club and carve it in from left to right, taking advantage of the extra spin this would produce on the rock-hard surface. It would be especially challenging from a ball above his feet.

He engaged the Pre-Set swing and the four-count rhythm, sending the five-iron fade towering toward the left side of the hole, cutting back to the audacious pin. The jet black clouds of the impending storm provided a surreal backdrop to his white ball arcing through the sky. I could tell from the sound of the ball coming off his club-face and his smile that he liked what he felt. The crowd began to scream uncontrollably as the ball crashed into the green with several thousand RPMs of backspin, causing its first and second bounces to skid like a drag racer. It then spun wildly to the right as it put its flaps down and caught the slope towards the hole. The noise was deafening as the ball came to rest four feet left of the hole. He would have a short but ticklish putt.

TK tossed his club to his caddy and graciously acknowledged the crowd by tipping his hat, all the while smiling. No one had seen him smile on the golf course before this day. He then spontaneously jogged over and gave my caddy a hefty high five that nearly knocked over his wheelchair. They shared a laugh as TK pointed toward him to acknowledge his sacrifice to the crowd. The decibels increased another level as TK grabbed the soldier's hand and held it high. It was an inspiring storybook scene.

I knew that this display of unbridled joy would be seen by many as inappropriate behavior and unbecoming a professional. But something deep inside told me that it would be OK in the end, and that this moment's true purpose was to celebrate the total sacrifice of our hero and the uncommon freedom birthed this day in both him and TK.

TK was unleashed. He was living fully and playing from the heart, not the prison cell of the past. We began the long walk around the canyon to the showdown on the green, all the while pushing the wheelchair of the true hero.

TK smiled and said, "That's for tricking me on 16!"

The crowds were huge and wild. This sport had never seen anything like this. An overnight transformation had descended upon the game. It would never be the same. The fans knew they were a part of history. This Ryder Cup-like fan reaction became the norm on the PGA Tour. It was as though Arnie's Army was back in full force. Those watching would refer back to the U.S. Open of this year as the line in the sand for the future of golf, and it had nothing to do with technology. It had everything to do with a new strain of soul freedom.

We received a standing ovation as we broke through the trees and walked up to the green side by side, pushing the soldier's chair. It was as though there wasn't a crowd favorite. We were being cheered on in the same sense as a team. The moment was glorious; we were living our dream in more ways than one. TK's hand was raised as he acknowledged the fans then all of the sudden he dropped it and the look of freedom was replaced by the look of shock and pain. It was as though a lightning bolt of his past had struck. He had indeed seen a ghost.

"You good?" I asked as TK's eyes began to glaze over.

"Without looking obvious, look over at the alleyway leading to the scorers' tent," he said, while trying to force a smile for the crowd.

I glanced over as we continued to walk to the edge of the green. There was a scowling Asian gentleman in his corporate uniform standing among several of TK's many handlers. This man looked angry and on a mission in his suit and tie.

"That your agent?" I asked, assuming his team didn't like this new swing and attitude.

TK's caddy set down his bag, TK grabbed his towel and whipped his face, not for the sweat, but the pain. He then grabbed his putter and looked at me and said, "No, it's worse. That's my father."

My mind began to race as I thought back to Grace's story of that fateful day when TK was 13. But something else quickly entered my mind. It was the story Johnny had read. TK's dad wasn't the dream-taker if Johnny's words were correct. He was but a scapegoat for the enemy that stole his heart somewhere along the way.

TK headed out to mark his ball. I began to wheel my caddy out on the green to my ball so that he could help me read the putt. TK tossed his ball to his caddy as we were about to pass him. The crowd had quieted and the tournament had come down to this dramatic finish.

Emotional chaos was exploding in TK's mind and soul. And I was feeling the effects. TK had tasted freedom but the sight of his dad slammed the door to the prison once again. I was compelled by the Almighty to an audacious call.

"TK, this is your defining moment," I courageously said as I stopped and stared him down. "And it has nothing to do with a putt for the U.S. Open."

And just like that, two potential U.S. Open champions were locked in a conversation on a stage in front of millions.

"What do you mean, Luke," TK asked as we both tried to look inconspicuous as if we were discussing a ruling or something to do with golf.

"TK, your dad is not the enemy. He is a scapegoat for the true enemy. Somewhere along the way his dream was killed, and the thief is using him to kill yours. Freedom is yours, but you have to confront your dad, not with anger, but with compassion. He knows something you don't."

TK stared at me, then looked in the distance at the black hole of

146

the canyon as a thought storm brought flashbacks of pain. But then a glimmer of hope trumped the pain and fear. I could see revelation entering his mind as the pieces began to come together. Then he looked back at me, stunned at the 33:3 moment that had invaded his soul.

"Luke, you have no idea what you just did," he explained with resolve in his voice. "I have something I need to do that I should have done a long time ago."

"Go for it," I encouraged as I nodded in the direction of his father, knowing now was the time. "I will stall."

As I wheeled my caddy to my ball, TK handed his putter to his caddy then grabbed his cell phone out of his bag and headed toward his dad in the alleyway. He told the stunned official that he had an emergency message that came in before the round that he needed to share with his dad.

Meanwhile I had a 40-foot double-breaking downhill putt to win, or to get close for a playoff. Neither option looked possible at first glance. My caddy couldn't believe the conversation that he had overheard. On the way to the ball for comic relief he said, "So this is what players talk about inside the ropes?"

We both chuckled as we took a look at the break from behind the ball. We agreed this putt had to finish past the hole. Neither of us wanted to think about having to make a downhill slider on our second putt. I left the soldier behind the ball as I walked all the way to the other side of the hole to read it from there, but mostly to buy time for TK's mission.

In the meantime, TK ducked under the ropes and walked right up to his father. Before TK could open his mouth his dad blurted out, "Why have you embarrassed and humiliated me?"

147

"Dad, it's your turn to stop talking and to listen." He paused as his eyes bore a hole through his father's bully posture. The crowd got still and quiet. TK just stood in the silence waiting for his dad to settle. "I will not return to that green to putt until you hear me out," he said as the storms intensified.

His dad, desperately wanting the victory for himself and his son, said, "OK, I'll listen."

The rules official tapped TK on the shoulder and said that he needed to return to the green soon since it was almost his turn. TK's dad looked panicked, but TK never took his eyes off his dad and told the rules official he was sorry but he would be there shortly. He continued as the crowd leaned in to eavesdrop on this extraordinary event.

"Dad, I have something to show you," TK said as he pulled up the screen saver on his phone. It was an exquisite pencil sketch of a magnificent black stallion running free. Though it was a drawing, it seemed to move. It was so real, so detailed, it almost jumped off the page.

TK's dad stared as his frenetic world stopped spinning. The sketching absorbed his every emotion and his knees became weak. He put his hand on his son's shoulder to steady his balance and then meekly asked, "Where did you get that?"

TK replied, "I found it by accident several years ago while looking for something in your closet. There was an entire box full of sketches hidden in the back of your closet. I took a picture of this one on my phone."

The tears began to flow as his dad stared at the horse. "Your granddad worked hard in Korea to send me to America to become a petroleum engineer. I would be the first of our family to ever go to college. I wanted to be an artist. Dad had forbidden me to draw, saying there was no money in it, no future. He said the responsible thing to do was to get an engineering degree, a traditional job, and to be extraordinary at it. I chose a school in Texas so that I could see horses. They represented freedom to me. I took every chance I could to sneak off campus and sketch horses for hours. After you were born, I continued to sketch while you and your mother went to church on Sundays. It was fuel for my soul. In the end I was forced to bury my art in a box because of the strain of leading the business. That was my last sketch, probably 10 to 12 years ago."

"Dad," TK said, "I am an artist like you. I expressed my art through creativity in how I played this game. At the age of 13 you killed my dream by forcing me to become a robot, and you almost ruined my teacher's life."

"Yes, I remember. Something in me snapped that day," TK's dad said with a pained expression on his face. "I became enraged. It wasn't about Johnny or you. It was about me and my dad and a lost passion. I never watched you play because I buried my pain in my work; it was my escape. I used Johnny as the scapegoat for my pain. I blamed him as a threat to your future and the traditions of the game. But really I was trying to keep art buried. I rationalized that I was protecting you as my dad did for me. But really what I was doing was justifying the death of my dream by killing yours and getting Johnny out of the way."

"Dad," TK whispered through tears of his own. "I forgive you. I love you."

There was a long embrace as the stunned crowd witnessed the reconciliation of a broken relationship.

149

Finally, after a few moments, TK's dad said, "I can see after today's performance that I was wrong. You are indeed my son the artist. You have my DNA. I didn't think I would ever be able to say this, but I am proud of you and happy that you had the courage to break the bond of fear. I am so sorry that I didn't have that same courage and that I nearly killed your dreams."

"It is time for both of us to pursue our passion," TK responded. "The world needs your art, and I need the father that I never had."

"Maybe you're right," TK's dad said with new life expressed with a cautious smile.

They both looked over to the green and halted their conversation as I approached my putt from 40 feet.

I faced the hole with the Face-On putter. It felt comfortable and secure even though I had only been putting in this manner for a little over a month. Looking at the hole was so helpful in judging the distance. My stroke felt like a pendulum, sending the ball on a painfully slow trek toward a U.S. Open victory. It took the first break just as we thought, then began to pick up speed as it was tumbling toward the hole. It took the second break, making a line for the hole. My heart was pounding as I took a step toward the hole about to raise my putter in victory. Then, the ball's momentum kept it from finishing the break, and it rolled past the hole to the gasps of the crowd, stopping about six feet below the hole. My caddy and I both carefully watched its path as it went by the hole, thus solidifying the read coming back.

Glancing at TK as I wheeled my caddy across the green to my ball, I saw a smile on both his and his dad's face. TK slightly held up 2 fingers by his side and nodded letting me know he was almost done but needed a little more time. My heart soared at the thought that TK had his heart back and maybe his father.

I was still out, so once again I took the maximum amount of time to read the putt. I slowly looked at it from both sides. I had to laugh inside at the irony of the situation. I had a putt that most only dream of, yet I was stalling to protect my competitor. This was beautiful.

TK re-engaged with his father. "I died inside at the age of 13 when you killed my dream and took away my teacher," he continued. "Even though I have become number one in the world, there is no life inside. I live as a prisoner. I want my freedom back, but most of all I want my dad back."

TK's dad nodded in understanding while wiping his eyes on his sleeve.

"So here is what is going to happen," TK leaned in so he could whisper into his father's ear so that no one else could hear. "Cancel all your meetings; tomorrow there is a good chance you are going on an adventure with me. The destination is a secret. And from now on, I will choose how I will play the game. I would rather play with freedom and lose than to win and feel trapped. Freedom is a powerful force."

His dad whispered back, "But what about the potential of a play-off?"

TK winked at his dad as he returned to the green. There was a noticeable murmur moving through the crowd as the story spread. This was better than Hollywood.

While TK had been finishing up his time with his father, I had marked my ball and tossed it to my caddy, not because it needed to be cleaned but as another stall tactic. The soldier noticed my hand shaking as I reached for the ball after he'd cleaned it.

"Ain't no one shooting at you," he encouraged. "It's just a putt! You know how to do that, right?" I broke into a smile as we confirmed that it was a firm, right-center putt.

TK had walked back over to his completely confused and shaken caddy who handed him his putter. I knelt down and took one last look from behind the ball. I was lining up my six-footer to possibly win the U.S. Open. This was the moment of childhood make-believe come to life.

The thunder was more frequent in the distant and the sky becoming darker by the minute. The wind shifted slightly from the north, bringing cool relief from the relentless heat. You could smell a hint of rain in the air. I shivered like I had at the Obra Maestra when the Spirit had invaded that moment.

I finally approached the putt of my life, yet I had no fear. I stood over the putt and looked up at TK, who was about 10 feet away. I quoted one of Johnny's favorite scriptures, "Perfect love casts out all fear." He nodded in understanding. I stroked the ball into the center of the cup.

TK smiled big and said, "Great putt." He proceeded to carefully look over his putt. It was a tricky side-hiller that would take steady nerves. He approached the putt face-on and stroked a beautiful putt that curved perfectly to the bottom of the cup for a U.S. Open tie. The crowd roared in appreciation for our play and seemingly would not stop. There would be an 18-hole playoff the following day to determine the U.S. Open champion. At least that was the traditional way of settling a tie in the U.S. Open.

TK embraced me like a long-lost friend and thanked me for saving his life. A huge gust of wind from the approaching storm came sweeping across the green, blowing trash and hats in all directions.

We quickly headed for the scorers' tent after heartfelt handshakes and hugs from the caddies. I embraced my soldier caddy and thanked him for coaching me to the finish. Sky then whisked him and the clubs to shelter.

The U.S. Open required an 18-hole playoff the following day. However, the severe thunderstorms and possible tornadoes that were advancing quickly were expected to rage through the night and into the middle of the week. Loudspeakers implored the relentlessly applauding spectators to leave immediately as tournament volunteers ushered people to the exits as quickly as possible. The maintenance crews rushed to "batten down the hatches" as the weather radar confirmed that the golf course was right in the bull's-eye of these fast approaching and dangerous storms.

On the way up the alleyway TK asked if I was willing to agree to a tie if the course was rendered unplayable the next day due to the storms. It would be a first in the history of the Open. I agreed without hesitation. We then spoke to the lead official in the scorer's tent. We all agreed that if the predicted dangerous storms struck the area, both the spectators and volunteers would have more important issues to deal with than a golf tournament. In that worst-case scenario, we agreed that a tie would be declared.

After we signed our cards, officials cancelled post-round interviews so everyone could get to safety. TK and I were hustled off to our hotel by a police escort. On our ride to the hotel he proposed an idea that brought a smile to my face and would forever intrigue the world of golf.

● Johnny's U.S. Open ●

Chapter 16

As anticipated, the storms wreaked havoc through the night. Tornado sirens blared one after another as a series of tornadoes and straight-line winds ripped through northeastern Oklahoma with more on the way. The morning greeted folks with devastation in several neighborhoods and a golf course that looked like a war zone. Bleachers and hospitality tents were twisted and strewn about the fairways from a series of straight-line winds, the creek had changed into a raging river, and baseball-sized hail stones had shredded the leaves from the trees and rendered the greens unplayable. This town had more pressing issues than concluding a U.S. Open.

The phone call came early with the official word: In an unprecedented move, the tournament committee had declared a tie.

As planned, TK and I met his dad at a local jet port where his plane had just arrived. Most of the private jets had escaped to Dallas the night before to avoid storm damage. TK had also invited a legendary golf writer to join us. Because the post-round interviews had been cancelled and a tie declared, this writer would have an exclusive and intriguing story to report.

We flew to the nearest airport to Utopia where Johnny picked us up. TK's dad, in a posture of complete humility, offered up a humble and heartfelt apology to Johnny. Johnny's grace was beyond comprehension. He embraced TK's dad as if he were a long-lost friend. He forgave him as God forgives us. Then the tears of joy streamed down Johnny's face when he gave TK a bear hug saying, "Welcome home."

TK and I teed off at the Links of Utopia to determine the unofficial winner of the U.S. Open. There were three men watching: Johnny, TK's dad, and the golf writer.

Before the first shot was struck, TK gave his dad a present wrapped in brown paper held together with twine. TK's dad was delighted by the gift. He opened it, finding a sketchpad and drawing pencil that brought tears to his eyes and fuel to the flickering light of a hidden dream in his soul. This makeshift and unprecedented playoff would be recorded for all future generations through the sketches of this book and the words written by our golf writer friend.

Johnny appointed himself the rules official. We played with Johnny's antique hickory shafted clubs. My ball was marked with SFT, and TK's with OM, to Johnny's delight. By the way, we improved our lies, took mulligans off the first tee, gave putts inside the leather, created our own holes a few times, and various other things that were common and accepted practice at the Links of Utopia. After all, as Johnny our rules official agreed, the entire course was declared "ground under repair," to put it mildly.

We entered the zone of pure and undefiled fun, the foundation of backyard sport. It is a shame that organized sport has stolen the heart and imaginations of our children. The word sandlot has become obsolete in a generation in need of magical moments.

At the end of this glorious day of fun and uninhibited competition, we were tied going into 18. As we approached the short, par-five 18th, we could see in the distance a large crowd of Utopians gathering around the green. Next to the green and the small pond were two saddled horses, Picasso and the regal black stallion that had recently found freedom. TK and I both reached the green in two to the loud applause of the country folks. Our approach shots had each come to rest near the same spot, about 25 feet from the hole.

Meanwhile, TK's dad had climbed up on a large rock that jutted out into the small man-made lake next to the green to sketch the horses. Both horses were standing next to the water. He was creatively sketching their reflections in the water when something caught his eye. His reaction began with one lone tear but turned into a flood of emotion as the revelation hit. The supernatural descended upon the natural for him for the first time.

The OM brand on the black stallion, which came from Old McDonald Breeders near Houston was magnified in the reflection of the water. It was the same mark TK had been using on his golf ball for the past two days.

TK joined his dad for this intimate moment. His dad asked him to show him the sketch on his phone. He asked him to zoom in on the brand on the black stallion in the sketch. As he did, the faint OM brand became visible. Then he asked him to zoom in on the lone white foot. When he did, they looked up at the stallion and were speechless.

Grace appeared out of the crowd, walking toward Johnny. They hugged and then walked arm and arm to the horses where they met TK and his dad. Grace cried as she hugged her friend TK that she hadn't seen or heard from in 10 years. He was visibly moved. She then smiled at TK's father and embraced him as well.

Johnny said, "Grace has something she wants to share with you."

"These are your horses; we have just been holding them for you." She said.

To TK she said, "Let me introduce you to Obra Maestra."

She handed the reins of the majestic black stallion to a deeply moved and stunned TK.

She turned over the reins of the paint horse to TK's father and said with a smile, "This is Picasso."

TK's dad starred into the eyes of Grace in disbelief. He held her gaze for a long time then choked out, "Why are you doing this? I hurt your family so much."

"That's one way to look at it," she replied as she patted Picasso. "But actually we are standing here today because of you. We are living our dream in Utopia."

She then paraphrased a scripture passage. "What was meant for harm, God turned to good. It's your turn for freedom, and these horses are a symbol to that gateway. They've been freed from their past. Today's your turn."

TK looked at Johnny with knowing in his eyes and said, "Johnny, Dad and I need to take a ride."

Johnny smiled and understood. "There's the trailhead son, follow the OM signs. He's been expecting you up on the mountain. Some sweet tea in the saddle bag."

"Who's up there?" asked TK's father.

"My favorite Artist," Johnny said with a smile and wink at TK.

They mounted their horses for a ride to the edge of heaven and to meet the Artist of grace.

Conclusion:

Johnny had dreamed about being a top-ten teacher many years ago. He thought that dream was dead, but on this day in the world's eyes he shattered it. I am sure it never entered his mind, because he had moved beyond the trivial and meaningless ratings from a pedestal-building society. He simply lived to teach and call out dreams. There has never been, nor will there ever be again, a teacher who coached two U.S. Open winners in the same year—and with non-traditional swings.

TK and I vowed to return to the 18th green of the Links of Utopia ten years from that day to complete the unofficial U.S. Open playoff and to celebrate the stories of the sacred journey that would unfold between now and then. This would ultimately allow our future wives and children to share in this defining moment. This turn of events thrilled and intrigued our golf writer who couldn't wait to post his story both now and in ten years.

In the days that followed, Johnny had two holes cut in the 18th green, one for the day's flag, and one for the U.S. Open pin that remained in place from the day we suspended the outcome. This would allow every aspiring golfer who came through Utopia to attempt to make a putt to win the U.S. Open, the dream of every young golfer. Of course, Johnny's hope was that it would inspire every kid who came through to dream big, for that is what dream-guardians do.

And the U.S. Open pin… it was a six-foot bamboo pole with a red bandanna fastened at the top.

• Johnny's U.S. Open •

Epilogue:

Dream-Guardian… that's it. After two books and a movie, we can see it clearly now: Being a dream-guardian is Johnny's calling, which captivates a buried longing in our hearts, buried dream seed. He calls out greatness in us. He is a noticer who trusts God to give him insight into the dreams of a fellow traveler. He has the courage to call us out, to encourage us, and inspire us to "get in the game." He leads us on a journey of identifying then planting the dream seed. He has time for the interruptions of a hurting and searching humanity. Because he perceives people not as interruptions, but divine appointments, eternity is consistently changed.

Isn't that the longing of our soul: that our legacy, like Johnny's, leaves a footprint on eternity?

For each of you who have received inspiration from Johnny, there is an open invitation for you to join thousands who have taken the next step: Become a dream-guardian. Over 15,000 readers spontaneously created the start of this ongoing movement with the first book. They did it by distributing the book to 10 or more of their friends. That's well over 150,000 lives touched by the message of soul freedom. In every case, they were noticers who simply listened to the Voice as He led their steps and actions. Their Spirits were pricked about who needed this message at a moment in time… and another Johnny was born.

This movement has gained momentum and a name, "The Johnny Project." Ground zero for this stirring of the Spirit is in Augusta,

Georgia, home of The Masters. Isn't that just like God to use the epicenter of golf, for a purpose greater than man could conceive.

For you that have been called out as dream-guardians, head to *linksofutopia.com* and click on "The Johnny Project." You will find your multi-pack of either book waiting along with ideas on how to use your influence to inspire others to become Johnnies as well. You will also find curriculum for using the books in Sunday school, small groups, men's or women's fellowships, etc.

The *Links of Utopia* organization has one purpose: To provide support and encouragement to all the Johnnies out there who have the desire to become or continue to be dream-guardians in their spheres of influence. We would love for you to join us on a retreat in Utopia. What a privilege to trek with you along the narrow yet adventurous path to true north.

Coming soon:

Be looking for books about the *Utopia Pre-Set*, the *Psychology of Tournament Golf*, *Face-On Putting*, *Life's Sacred Journey*, and going *Beyond Success*. You will find information regarding these and other resources at *linksofutopia.com*. There is also an on-line store featuring *SFT* products as well.

About the Author:

Dr. David L. Cook is an author, speaker, entrepreneur, and mental training coach. Golf Digest (2013) named him one of the Top Ten mental game experts in golf. His clients have included PGA Tour winners, NBA World Champions and MVPs, Olympians, National Collegiate Champions, and many Fortune 500 companies. He served as President and Chairman of the Board for Utopia Films, the production company for the movie *Seven Days in Utopia* starring Robert Duvall. He also co-wrote the screenplay and served as an Executive Producer. David is a Baylor graduate and received his Ph.D. in Sport and Performance Psychology from the University of Virginia. He and his wife Karen have two daughters and live in the Hill Country of Texas.

For inquiries regarding Dr. Cook's speaking availability please contact Ambassador Speaker's Bureau at ambassadorspeakers.com.

Folds of Honor:

For inquiries about *Folds of Honor* organization that was spoken about in Chapter 12, please go to foldsofhonor.org. This distinquished organization deserves the attention and support of all of us that enjoy our freedom. The magnificent Patriot Club is a real course just outside of Tulsa and the *Folds of Honor* organization is housed on the property.